Cyberschools:

An Education Renaissance

http://www.cyberschools.com

Also by Glenn R. Jones

Make All America a School

*Jones Cable Television and Information
Infrastructure Dictionary*

*Briefcase Poetry
Volumes 1-3*

Cyberschools:
An Education Renaissance

http://www.cyberschools.com

Glenn R. Jones

With a Foreword by Alvin and Heidi Toffler

Jones Digital Century, Inc.
Englewood, Colorado

JONES DIGITAL CENTURY, INC.
A DIVISION OF JONES INTERNATIONAL,™ LTD.
9697 E. MINERAL AVENUE, ENGLEWOOD, CO 80112

Portions of *Cyberschools* appeared previously in *Make All America a School*, published in 1991 by Jones 21ST Century, Inc., a division of Jones International,™ Ltd., 9697 E. Mineral Avenue, Englewood, CO 80112.

ISBN: 1-885400-67-5

Library of Congress Catalog Card No.: 96-95291

Imagination is the most powerful human resource on the planet. Harnessing it and its resultant electronic tools in the service of education is the great hope of the world. This book is dedicated to the people who will make it happen.

ABOUT THE AUTHOR

GLENN R. JONES is founder and chief executive officer of Jones International, Ltd., whose subsidiaries have been leaders in cable television since 1961 and in electronically delivered distance education since 1987.

Mr. Jones has served on the board of directors of the National Cable Television Association (NCTA), Cable in the Classroom and C-SPAN, and on the boards of the National Alliance of Business (NAB) and the American Society for Training and Development (ASTD). He is founder of the Global Alliance for Transnational Education (GATE).

Mr. Jones has received awards for advancing minorities and women in media. He also has received several honorary doctoral degrees.

A graduate of the University of Colorado School of Law and the Stanford University Business School Executive Program, Mr. Jones is the author of *Make All America a School, The Jones Dictionary of Cable Television Terminology,* and several volumes of poetry.

CONTENTS

TOWARD A LEARNING COMMUNITY ON THE PLANET

There are people who contribute greatly to society by thinking small — by focusing intensely on a set of narrow, sometimes incredibly complex, problems and working to solve them. There are others who contribute equally — and sometimes more — by thinking big. They tackle vast recalcitrant, even more complex problems. Some, of course, do nothing but talk big dreams. Others work long and hard to make them come true and, for their trouble, are often dismissed as cranks, dreamers or idealists. Some are. A few, however, are just the reverse.

Glenn Jones is one of these. A successful, hard-headed businessman, he has built a large, important cable TV, telecommunications, and new media company starting from absolute scratch. That would be dream enough for most people. But Jones believes that the most successful businesses of the future — bigger and more profitable than today's giants — will be those that help solve crucial social crises — environmental, health and, above all, the educational crisis.

While almost everyone is dissatisfied with existing schools, colleges and universities — not simply in the U.S. but across much of the world — most proposed innovations take for granted that educational problems can be solved within the existing framework.

Are our factory-style elementary and secondary schools in trouble? Increase homework. Increase teachers' pay. Patch up broken windows. In short, make the factory run faster.

Even as new technology and a Third Wave, knowledge-based economy move us from mass production of goods to customized or individualized production, children are still subjected to mass production education. (The idea of replacing the factory-style school with reconceptualized alternatives is still regarded as heresy by the educational establishment.)

Higher education, too, requires deep reconceptualization. Donald Langenberg, chancellor of the University of Maryland System and a former deputy director of the National Science Foundation, speculates that "many universities may die or may change beyond recognition as a result of the IT (information technology) revolution... Some may be 'virtual universities' that are delocalized across cyberspace." Which is what this book is about.

In public discourse, as in policy, "Education" with a capital E is regarded as a separate, specific category of social activity. "Media" are in another category. "Computers" are in still another category. Yet in the real world the boundaries among these categories are melting away. The world of computing and the world of media are converging. And it may be impossible to solve our most crucial social problems so long as we continue to think within the frame of these conventional categories.

Glenn Jones is a category-buster. And we believe, as he does, that education cannot be brought into the Third Wave future so long as it is viewed as separate from both the media and cyberspace.

In these pages, he lays out an exciting vision for the fusion of these activities into a new world-wide education revolution. There is no single panacea for our problems. What Glenn Jones proposes cannot be expected to solve all the accumulated problems of our obsolete educational assembly lines. But it does offer high-powered tools to help people — not only the rich in the rich countries, but all people — gain access to better education at lower cost as a Third Wave learning community begins to form around the planet.

— Alvin and Heidi Toffler

ACKNOWLEDGEMENTS

This book represents much of what I have learned about education, its complexity and the transforming impact that technology is bringing to it.

In my global quest to find the keys to merging technology with education, I have met hundreds of fellow pilgrims. They included many leaders in business and academia, professors, teachers, UNESCO officers, high technology practitioners, futurists, celebrities with educational perspectives and innumerable politicians and regulators around the globe. Without listing them individually, I sincerely acknowledge their contributions, for they have exhibited to me that there is good reason for hope in making all the world a school.

On a specific basis, however, I acknowledge my associates at the Jones Companies whose commitment to Jones Education Company (JEC™) and its subsidiaries, including JEC Knowledge TV™, JEC Knowledge Online™ and JEC College Connection™, has orchestrated the concept of *Cyberschools* into a marketable product. They are very special people and I thank them all, from Wally Griffin who oversaw JEC, to Jim O'Brien, Greg Liptak, Bob Hampton, David Zonker, Rich Nortnik and Elizabeth Steele, who are group-level officers at Jones, and all of my fellow associates reporting to them. I must also acknowledge good friends Don Sutton, a former Jones Associate, and Jim Ginsburg, along with Jim's wife Kimberley, who were especially instrumental in supporting the creation of Knowledge TV, and Dr. Bernard Luskin for his perspectives on distance education.

I greatly appreciate the support of my friends in the cable television industry who, among many contributions to education, gave the television network portion of our efforts life by carrying Knowledge TV. I must make special reference here to Time Warner for its ongoing cooperative spirit and backing and especially to TCI and John Malone for understanding what we were trying to do and giving us early, significant support.

Additionally, I would like to thank Jim Sample and Nancy Nachman-Hunt for their insights and their invaluable help in researching, refining and helping to organize, develop and polish the finished work; Sue Diehl for her professional and crucial copy editing; Debra Agnew and Mary Hill who worked diligently and patiently through the layout and production of numerous drafts; the excellent research staffs of the World Bank and the United Nations Education, Scientific and Cultural Organization which provided much of the education and population data; and Kim Dority, who helped prepare an earlier book, *Make All America A School*, from which grew *Cyberschools* and who provided early guidance and final review of the finished work.

Finally, I would like to acknowledge Ms. Dianne Eddolls, the lady in my life, for putting up with my intensity and the single-minded focus on *Cyberschools* that often consumed me.

There is only one good, knowledge, and one evil, ignorance.

—Socrates,
in *Diogenes Laertius*

INTRODUCTION

Since Socrates first addressed the nature of knowledge, educators have struggled with two central questions: what to teach and how to teach it. The debate echoes from antiquity and volleys across today's academic journals, government reports, business magazines, and mainstream best-sellers. Exploding beyond the borders of education and legislatures, the debate is now being enacted in town halls, corporate boardrooms, and even dining rooms throughout the world. The concept behind distance education offerings — frequently referred to as cyberschools in this book — is to deliver education to people instead of people to education.

This concept provides tested and proved answers to third and fourth questions: *Where* should the learning take place and *what* constitutes learning?

In our emerging global society, how these questions are answered has special significance because the answers will have a major impact on the many youthful, vibrant experiments with self-government, including the ongoing experiment with democracy in the United States. As historians Will and Ariel Durant pointed out more than two decades ago in *Lessons of History*, access to education is the key:

> If equality of educational opportunity can be established, democracy will be real and justified. For this is the vital truth beneath its catchwords: that though men cannot be equal, their access to educational opportunity can be made more nearly equal.[1]

Our global cultures have undergone a transformation that lends great urgency to these questions. This transformation is our headlong race through an information revolution to a knowledge-based society. This has created a sense that we are out of control. Decision-makers, who must in any event make decisions, are deluged with information they cannot grasp and with choices they do not comprehend. Everything is moving with great speed. There seems to be nothing to hold onto, and yet we must marvel at what is occurring.

Technology as a Transforming Force

In a process that may be unique in the history of mankind, we have created a technological capability that is transforming the global societies it touches. Land-line telephones in the early 1900s and television transmissions in the 1950s provide some rough context, but those technologies were quickly placed under the lock and key of traditional power interests. Perhaps the most important aspect of today's technology is that it proliferates beyond the control of traditional regulatory and industry cliques, though no small effort and expense are being expended to change that.

Most amazing, these changes have defied experts and pundits alike by progressing outside the bounds of any grand design, galvanized in many cases by the simple availability of fax machines, cable television, satellite TV dishes, computers with CD players, and Internet connections. The change has come about at the grassroots level of the world's societies, implemented by people using these new tools to communicate about how and why to accomplish the things they care about.

DEMAND FOR HIGHER EDUCATION

Because of the rapid rise in literacy and education levels in many countries, North American and Western European higher education have become stable and lucrative export products. In the United States, there is an ongoing, raucous debate over the quality of the country's education institutions, but other nations have no such concerns; in fact, almost a half million of the United States' 14 million university enrollees are from other countries. An educational inferiority complex has not squashed the desires of other countries' college-age students to obtain a U.S.-brand on their university diplomas.

These students are willing to travel great distances and in many cases commit themselves to years of government service in exchange for the financial support to enroll in traditional U.S. and European degree programs on campus. We must think about how the opportunities for these students, and millions more like them who do not have the financial means for overseas study, will exponentially expand if they can begin to receive the same quality and content of course work via electronic means, without the travel and at a fraction of the expense.

1 World Education Demand and Media Penetration		
	1985	**1992**
Students/K-Higher	986.9 million	1.1 billion
Students/Higher	58.6 million	73.7 million
Television Sets (per 1,000 pop.)	142	153
Daily newspapers (copies per 1,000 pop.)	95	96

Source: *World Education Report*, 1995; Statistical Division of the U.N., *Monthly Bulletin of Statistics*.

For example, this electronic capability will make it possible for the great Asian universities to reach out to the rest of the world that needs to improve its understanding of Asian culture.

The demand for electronic delivery of college courses should mushroom as we enter the 21st century. Our global society's rate of technological adaptation is both driving that demand and providing the tools to present education via electronic media.

WHAT THE KNOWLEDGE SOCIETY DEMANDS

To understand this chicken-and-egg phenomena, it is important to recognize some of the fundamental characteristics of our new knowledge society and the unique attributes that some Western-educated workers lend to this society.

The knowledge society we have entered differs greatly from the industrial society we leave behind. In the industrial society the principal resource was energy, and its tools were artifacts like forklifts, cranes, trucks, trains, automobiles, and airplanes. Its principal characteristic was that it allowed us to extend the human body.

The knowledge society is different because the velocity of its evolution is much more rapid, and its principal resource is information. Information is a special kind of resource. As has often been noted, it can be weightless, invisible, and in many different places at once. The tools of the information society drive the creation, storage, delivery, manipulation, and transformation of that information. Importantly, the principal characteristic of the knowledge revolution is that it allows us to dramatically extend the human mind by introducing a new model for learning.

The quantum extension of the human mind combined with the ability to extend the human body has resulted in a new reality. A reality in which the human mind, excluding religion and acts of nature, is now more clearly the most powerful force on the planet.

We are all embedded in this evolution, and education has an important part to play. Education is a process. Education is how information becomes meaningful. Information without meaning is useless. Education converts information into knowledge, understanding, and wisdom much like changing temperature turns water into ice. Education is the loom through which information is woven into value systems, dignity, self-worth, freedom and into civilization itself.

THE KNOWLEDGE WORKER

While all societies contribute to the evolution of education, economic and work force experts claim that the developed world's universities produce graduates with unique capabilities.

The emergence of the "knowledge worker" college graduate, as first defined by Peter F. Drucker in his 1959 book, *Landmarks of Tomorrow*[2], and later re-examined by Robert B. Reich in his 1991 book, *The Work of Nations: Preparing Ourselves for 21st Century Capitalism*, goes a long way toward describing the reasons why demand for the opportunity to receive Western college curriculum course content is so high.

The knowledge worker, or symbolic analyst as labeled by Reich, is that person who can produce new designs and concepts, as opposed to following standard procedures and producing familiar products.

Reich describes the demand for such an education:

Millions of people across the globe are trying to learn symbolic-analytic skills, and many are succeeding. Researchers and engineers in East Asia and Western Europe are gathering valuable insights into microelectronics, macrobiotics, and new materials, and translating these insights into new products. Young people in many developing nations are swarming into universities to learn the symbolic and analytic secrets of design engineering, computer engineering, marketing, and management.[3]

With the continuing deployment of these sought-after educational processes through distance learning and conventional classroom offerings, perhaps someday a society on a distant planet will seek to import the educational offerings which make possible our world's symbolic analyst learners.

A RENEWED FOCUS ON LEARNING

The evolution and continual specialization of our education processes in no way lessens the overall importance of education for the world as a whole. In fact, it intensifies it.

Will and Ariel Durant stated it well:

> If education is the transmission of civilization, we are unquestionably progressing. Civilization is not inherited; it has to be learned and earned by each generation anew; if transmission should be interrupted for one century, civilization would die, and we would be savages again. So our finest contemporary achievement is our unprecedented expenditure of wealth and toil in the provision of higher education for all.[4]

THE BRAIN UNDER SIEGE

The importance of general education is growing in tandem with the world's body of knowledge. Our libraries strain under the weight of books sounding the alarms of an information revolution and the speed at which new information is being generated.

By conservative estimate, the holdings of the world's libraries are doubling in volume every 14 years. At the end of the day, this information must be dealt with by an electrochemical contraption that weighs 3 pounds, more or less, takes up about half a cubic foot of space, runs on glucose at about 25 watts, processes information at the rate of approximately 100 quadrillion operations per second, looks like a big walnut, and is the world's first wet computer: the human brain. That brain is under siege, bombarded from all sides by torrents of new information.

The distance education approaches addressed in this book present an array of tools with which this vast body of knowledge may be considered, managed, and put to use by individuals. These tools can empower individuals through education by giving them the means to convert information into knowledge, understanding, and wisdom. They are technologies which can help spread out the decision–making process in governments, institutions, and businesses and empower the individual.

THE ROLE OF ELECTRONIC PLATFORMS

Technological advances such as cable TV and the Internet have created a communications environment where vast amounts of information can be delivered inexpensively, an environment where the barrier of distance is erased and the barrier of time is diminished. I refer to the companies that combine various forms of electronic information delivery as electronic platforms. The electronic platform is the new generation of media delivery organization, and the phenomena is rapidly finding adaptations in the education sector.

The distance education markets that are open because of technology are tremendous. If there are 50 students in an average classroom, then cable television's 62 million U.S. subscribers, multiplied by 2.5 people per home, represent a potential school with over 3 million classrooms. Cable TV can be of enormous help in today's information rich environment. An even bigger mass audience can be reached globally using the Internet, broadcasting, cable, and combinations of various technologies.

The television industry can respond to the world's education delivery needs, if its leaders will commit on several levels. Although cable television is improving the situation, society cannot afford an overall television environment that is entertainment rich and knowledge poor. According to media critic Duane Elgin, less than 5% of prime-time TV is typically devoted to informational programming. At the very time our democracies face problems of marathon proportions, we're preparing for that marathon with a diet of intellectual junk food.[5]

DEFINING EDUCATION

The convergence of technology with education has precipitated an active assault on the traditional concept of learning.

Certainly the "out of control" school of alarmists have reason to be concerned. While technology provides wonderful opportunities for communication, research, and multimedia displays, it is also available to those who can — and do — abuse it under the name of "education."

Diploma mills have proliferated for over 300 years and now can dispense ad hoc degrees-on-a-disk or doctorates by e-mail. And, racing to shelter under the education umbrella, TV executives claim that all they do is in the name of learning and furthering viewers' cultural horizons.

Is all information education? Possibly.

Should all information be accorded similar levels of respect and credence by education and media organizations? Unequivocally, no.

Just as college credits are sometimes inappropriately given to students for completely irrelevant "life experience," a broadcast of "The Sword of Zorro" as an education program represents an abuse.

At the same time, education and consumer groups alike should expect and demand reasonable and expedient open certification of distance education offerings. To pretend that it does not matter, that certification will be granted in due time, is to invite failure in our response to the needs of the world's rapidly growing class of 21st century lifelong learners.

We are blazing through an information revolution that is technology-driven. If we don't measure up to the responsibilities of leadership in the knowledge content we select and develop to distribute through our new technology, the knowledge society that awaits us will fall far below its potential.

Revolutions are transitory. Though it may come as a surprise to many media and technology zealots, the information revolution is already in its waning days. Technologies will continue to be invented and to proliferate, but the fundamental restructuring of the world's economic and political systems already has been set in motion. We have the result rapidly unfolding around us, a knowledge-based society which is the legacy ascendant of the revolution.

THE CRITICAL ISSUE: SPEED

Critical issues must be addressed about ensuring the quality of our education processes and content. Fortunately, our current focus has come to be not on avoiding an interruption of its delivery, but rather on how quickly and effectively it can be delivered.

The issue was stated in clear economic terms by William B. Johnston and Arnold H. Packer in their landmark study *Workforce 2000*, which cited education and training as the primary systems by which human capital is both developed and protected.[6] The speed and efficiency with which these same systems transmit knowledge and influence the rate of human capital growth is more important than the traditional gauge of rate of investment in plant and equipment, the same study noted.

It is the obligation and opportunity of every person and organization committed to the concept of self-government and to the forward progress of civilization to lend what tools they can to assist in the education of humankind. The questions are what, how, where, and when to teach for optimum benefit, optimum benefit to individual learners, to the concept of self-government, and to the forward progress of civilization.

THE LESSON OF ATHENS

Imagine the vibrant energy and intellect of Athens during the time of Socrates and Plato. The ghost of Athens is visible today, but it also represents a lesson about missed opportunity that should not be lost on the TV broadcasting, cable, and telephony industries.

According to Plato, when the Athenians decided they didn't want to give to society, but wanted society to give to them, when the freedom they wished for most was freedom from responsibility, then Athens ceased to be free.

It has been said that Plato, in all his strivings to imagine an ideal training school, failed to notice that Athens itself was a greater school than even he could dream of.

Let us notice *our* environment. It is time now to fuse our knowledge society electronic tools with our great teaching institutions and information repositories. It is time to create a world that is, like Athens was, a great school, a world vibrant with interest and excitement about education, a world where educational opportunity is visible to all and hope is alive, a world that sees the wilderness of information as our new frontier.

[1]Will and Ariel Durant, *The Lessons of History* (New York: Simon and Schuster, 1968), 79.

[2]Peter F. Drucker, *Landmarks of Tomorrow* (New York: Harper & Row, 1959).

[3]Robert B. Reich, *The Work of Nations: Preparing Ourselves for 21st Century Capitalism* (New York: Alfred A. Knopf, 1991), 225.

[4]W. and A. Durant, *Lessons of History*, 101.

[5]Duane Elgin, "Sustainable Television," *In Context* (January 1990), 27.

[6]William B. Johnston and Arnold H. Packer, *Workforce 2000: Work and Workers for the Twenty-first Century* (Indianapolis, Ind.: Hudson Institute, 1987), xxvii.

**There is no domestic knowledge and
no international knowledge. There is
only knowledge.**

—Peter F. Drucker,
  in *The Atlantic Monthly*

THE GLOBAL EDUCATION CHALLENGE

The dawning of any century can be counted upon to elicit prophecies and prognostications from all manner of philosophers, poets, and pontificators. For the world of higher education, the predictions are that schools and universities worldwide are going to be faced with educating more people with fewer dollars for longer periods of time and then finding them back again a few years later for more.

History provides the evidence that these forecasts are right. In essence, higher education in the 21st century will find itself playing a game of catch up.

The destruction and death wrought by World War II in Europe, Asia, and Africa left those continents and their societies years behind in their development of key competencies, including education infrastructure and programs. Beginning in the late 1960s — reflecting the 20-plus years it took for many countries just to produce new college-age generations — the world's education institutions began to respond to new demands.

The following three decades saw the demand for education evolve at an alarming rate. Between 1985 and 1992 alone, the world's total student body, pre-school through all types of higher education, grew by 119.7 million, from 986.9 million to 1.1 billion. That's a 12% increase in just seven years.[1]

2 World Education — Vital Statistics			
	1985	**1992**	**% change**
Population	4.9 billion	5.5 billion	12
Students/K-Higher*	986.9 million	1.1 billion	12
Students/Higher*	58.6 million	73.7 million	26
% of World's GNP for Education	4.9%	5.1%	0.2

Source: *World Education Report*, 1995; Statistical Division of the U.N., *Monthly Bulletin of Statistics*. *Includes all types of post-high school education.

3 World Literacy			
	1980	**2000 (projected)**	**% increase**
World	69.6%	79.4%	9.8
Developed Countries	96.6%	98.9%	2.3
Developing Countries	58%	73.4%	15.4
China	66%	85%	19
India	40.8%	55.8%	15

Source: *World Education Report*, 1995.

There also has been a tremendous and encouraging increase in the enrollments of primary and secondary students, particularly in developing countries, and the world's literacy level is improving steadily. Most astounding is that the number of students seeking higher education — including vocational training and university certificate and degree programs — grew 26% during the same seven-year period, adding 15.1 million students. That's the highest growth rate of any single education sector.

Driven by world population growth, improving literacy rates, and desire for growth in personal incomes, the demand for higher education continues to grow. During the 1985-92 period, the number of students enrolled in secondary education programs grew 14%, from 294 million to 334 million,[2] and some education analysts anticipate that at least 30% of these secondary-level students will want some form of higher education by the early 21st century.

4 World Higher Education Student Growth			
	1985	**1992**	**% change**
Asia	17.6 million	24.9 million	42
Europe/Russia Fed.	17.0 million	19.0 million	12
North America	13.9 million	16.4 million	18

Source: *World Education Report,* 1995.

THE NEW ADULT LEARNER

But secondary school graduates are by no means the only segment of the world's population seeking higher education. Let's look at how the world's student body has changed over the past generation.

Our past assumptions about who the typical college student was and how, what, when, why, and where that student attended college are no longer valid. Today the world's colleges and universities are faced with new student body demographics. This trend coincides with the arrival of the digital age.

There are at least three typical global higher education student profiles. One is Asian as its dominant trait; another is over 23 years of age; and the third holds an associate-equivalent or bachelor's degree and either has been or is about to be "downsized" from a job.

These student profiles share two common traits: Their current educational pursuits include a heavy component of technology-related courses — engineering, healthcare, or computer — and they are paying a significant portion of their tuitions out of their own pockets via personal savings, loans, or assistance from their families.

In addition, as the average college student age of 23 indicates, we no longer define a college education as something we do between the ages of 18 and 22. We are coming to understand and embrace the concept of "lifelong learning."[3] Indeed, lifelong learning has moved from the category of "discretionary" personal investment to "essential" as people scramble to bolster their credentials in a volatile global workplace.

Upward mobility through education is not just a tactic of white-collar management and computer professionals, either. The range of professions looking for education options goes from nurse practitioners to golf course groundskeepers and from sanitation and environmental technicians to assistant chefs.

For a number of reasons, one being an aging Western population and another being the view outside the industrialized world that college education is an import, versus export, industry, many countries now are turning their attention to providing education that will keep their college students and their education dollars at home, rather than shipping them out to Los Angeles or Paris.

Yet another interesting dimension to the growing demand for education is that although the developing world's student population is young, the priorities placed on education and continued improvement by all societies suggest that this large and rapidly growing young student body represents a long-term market for lifelong learning programs.

Some education authorities describe the "bubble" of Western baby boomers who are demanding lifelong learning options as though it is a phenomenon that might disappear into retirement homes in the next 30 years.

This is a mistake.

The faulty assumption that, within a generation or so, the world's student bodies will have returned to traditional college campuses as the only bona fide education source both fails to take into account the characteristics of the rest of the world's lifelong learners and the societal and economic forces that will drive them over the next 20 years.

At the very least, lifelong learners among the Western baby boomers will soon be joined and eventually eclipsed by seekers of education from developing countries in both East and West Asia and, eventually, Africa.

To meet both the short-term and long-term demand, countries must either build universities and staff them with world-class faculty or augment their higher education institutions with less expensive alternatives. Distance education — the delivery of education courses from one location to students at another location — is an alternative. Within distance education, cyberschools are a relatively new concept because they represent education content and classes that are conducted electronically, and they are definitely an economical option.

PUBLIC FINANCING

Cyberschools appear at an opportune moment in history. Statistics show that public financing for education the world over is shrinking. In the late 1980s and early 1990s public financing to support the global education system grew in total outlay, but at a much slower rate than demand. Despite the rapid influx of students, governments and taxpayers worldwide increased support to education by only 0.2% of their Gross National Products.

Part of that low rate of increase can be attributed to demand outstripping supply, but even more of it can be assigned to antiquated models for building education infrastructure. Some education leaders insisted that education at all levels — and accredited courses in particular — be delivered only by providing traditional bricks-and-mortar campuses with class ratios and class environments approved by faculty committees and administrators. These education Luddites have completely missed the boat in understanding the type of global societal change driving education demand and what must be done to respond to it.

The quality of educational content and delivery has been and should always be the first concern. Likewise, there always will be a place for traditional campuses and classroom settings. But 21st century students will need varied classroom environments and diverse education delivery systems. There is no one way courses must be taught, so long as students learn and can demonstrate their learning through accredited testing and examination procedures.

Globally, fiscal concerns will increasingly drive the delivery of education. Shrinking fiscal support for education in developed and developing countries alike makes it crucial that new models for education incorporate delivery by both traditional institutions and carefully integrated electronic platforms. (The term electronic platform, as it applies to education, refers to the technology that makes possible electronic delivery using any of a wide array of telecommunications systems, including, without limitations, broadcast, satellite, cable television, radio, telephone, computer, and the Internet.)

5 1995 Global GNP Growth & Higher Education Students

Country	GNP +	Population in millions	% in Higher Ed.	Students in millions
China	11.8%	1,210	0.2%	2.5
Korea	7.6%	45	4.0%	1.8
Japan	0.6%	125	3.4%	4.2
Thailand	8.6%	59	1.2%	0.7
Malaysia	8.4%	20	1.0%	0.2
Indonesia	6.7%	207	0.1%	1.9
Philippines	4.3%	75	2.5%	1.9
India	5.0%	952	2.2%	21.3
United States	3.3%	300	4.7%	14.0

Source: World Bank, Pacific Economic Cooperation Council, and analysts' estimates.

A comparison of GNP growth with 1995 rates of population enrolled in higher education throughout the world suggests an imminent explosion in additional demand.

Although the level of public financing for higher education has plateaued in many countries and in some countries has even decreased concurrently with unprecedented demand for education, alarmed pundits ignore three crucial facts:

- First, students of enormously varying financial means are finding ways to attain higher levels of education, often without the public financing support of a decade ago.

- Second, in this era of public budget deficits, public financing for education is constrained and certainly is not likely to increase at the same rate as the demand for education, no matter how shrill the alarms. The private sector, from small private universities and polytechnics to electronic colleges offering on-line courses and degrees, is already offering alternatives.

- Third, in many cases, especially with developing countries, public funds are being redirected to pre-primary, primary, and secondary education programs and away from higher education in an effort to improve basic literacy and student income-producing capability. This change in priorities is supported by both World Bank and UNESCO education study recommendations.[4]

There is good reason to argue that public funding cannot, and need not, keep pace, even at the secondary level.

The United States in particular probably spent too many dollars on education programs during the 1970s and 1980s, with dubious benefits in some cases.

A special report on world education published by *The Economist* magazine in 1992 noted that while the United States had the highest level of per-pupil public dollars — about $6,000 per student — for primary and secondary students of all the industrialized nations, it also had the highest level of high school dropouts at 14% and a notoriously under-qualified fledgling work force. U.S. university students and graduates ranked somewhat better, albeit with less dependency on public funding. Japan and Germany both spent far less in public funds educating their students with better results in terms of work-force skills, the report noted.[5]

Throwing public funds at the U.S. education problem, *The Economist* editors concluded, does not seem to be a prescription for success.

At the higher education level, high costs also are contentious and have reached the point of limiting access. One partial solution to the financial access barrier is to adopt additional ways to augment the higher education railroad, so to speak, ways that include the use of technology available through private-sector educational alternatives.

LESSONS FROM THE WORLD BANK

In 1994, the International Bank for Reconstruction and Development (IBRD), part of the World Bank, released *Higher Education: The Lessons of Experience*, a report that spelled out the bank's successes and failures in helping underwrite higher education in developing countries. Noting that direct investments in traditional higher education had sometimes produced disappointing or hard-to-define results, the report lauded distance learning approaches in developing countries:

> Distance education and open learning programs can be effective in increasing access, at modest cost, for underprivileged groups that are usually poorly represented in university enrollments...distance education can be an effective way also to provide lifelong education and upgrade skills, as when used for in-service teacher training. [Since 1970] distance education has

rapidly expanded in Bangladesh, China, India, Indonesia, Korea, Pakistan, the Philippines, Sri Lanka, and Thailand. [Thailand's two open universities] have been the government's principal instrument for expanding access to students from the poorest social strata, especially in urban areas. Operating on a self-financing basis, the open universities account for 62% of Thailand's higher education enrollments. Distance education programs can also be designed with a regional (multinational) clientele. For example, UNISA, the Open University of South Africa, draws 15,000 of its 120,000 students from neighboring countries.[6]

Such programs, the report noted, are usually much less expensive than conventional university programs because of much higher student-teacher ratios.

The report stated there was an international higher education crisis: shrinking funds to meet a growing demand. It discussed various cause and effect factors, but pinpointed two key facets of the crisis:

- Developing countries that had funded higher education to the detriment of primary and secondary education were not experiencing comparable increases in jobs requiring college degrees; and

- Funds for higher education in most countries were decreasing, especially government-funded degree and grant programs, placing more students in the status of self-reliant.[7]

While deploring the decline in funding for public education in most countries, the IBRD report noted that private institutions have been a key remedy in some countries, at little or no direct public cost.[8]

This is part of the evidence that, once above literacy and secondary-education levels, students will do their best to pay for their own educations and vocational and professional continuing study programs, providing these programs can be delivered at a reasonable cost. These are important points, too often played down when remedies to the public education crisis are sought, especially if public funding is involved.

Additionally, when institutions rely heavily on government funding, I think that their programs can sometimes reflect a to-be-expected, but unfortunate bias that does not necessarily reflect the interests of students.

Two years prior to IBRD's report on higher education, *The Economist* magazine's 1992 report had noted that educational reformers in developed countries were having a hard time coming up with solutions that budgets could solve, regardless of the availability of public funds.[9]

In any case, it is unlikely that financing from the public sector is going to experience a significant change. The better we understand the nature of the market demand for education and the more we recognize that higher funding is no sure-fire remedy for education at any level, the better our chances of applying cost-effective remedies that reflect present realities.

OLDER STUDENTS: BUDGET-MINDED LEARNERS

For at least some of the U.S. higher education establishment, economic reality is about to arrive in the form of a degreed student who must retrain to keep a job and doesn't have time or money for campus frills.

Enrollment of the "traditional" student in colleges and universities is dwindling. As late as 1979 in the United States, traditional full-time students, 18–22 years old and usually straight out of high school, numbered 4.5 million. By 1992, enrollment of traditional students was expected to fall from the 1979 high down to 3.1 million, a decline of 32%.[10]

As traditional students represent less and less of higher education's student body, however, adult learners are stepping in to fill the void. These students are typically 25–35 years old and are employed at least part time. Many of them have employers who are paying some or all of their education costs. These students deal with scheduling conflicts, difficulties in getting to campus, geographical relocation brought on by job transfers, and frequently the extra demands of parenthood.

Adult learners typically have little interest in the expensive "extras" of college such as social and athletic events, association with sororities or fraternities, and various other on-campus organizations and activities. They need flexible scheduling, affordable prices, and attendance options. In many cases, the existence of college libraries and bookstores are conveniences they will gladly forgo, providing they can receive reference materials and study assignments by postal service or, increasingly, over the Internet. Such students exist in all types and levels of education, and they are found virtually all around the globe.

Ken Dychtwald and Joe Flower in their book *Age Wave* described this changing approach to education:

> You may stop working one or more times in your thirties, forties, or fifties in order to go back to school, raise a second (or third) family, enter a new business, or simply to take a couple of years to travel and enjoy yourself. You may go back to work in your sixties, seventies, or even eighties. You may find that the traditional framework of life—with youth the time for learning, adulthood for non-stop working and raising a family, and old age for retirement—will come unglued, offering new options at every stage. A cyclic life arrangement will replace the current linear life plan as people change direction and take up new challenges many times in their lives.[11]

In fact, numerous studies undertaken in the past several years by industry groups, governments, public institutions, and private foundations are projecting that by the year 2020 the average worker will undergo *at least* five major job changes in his or her lifetime.

Germany and Japan present the most obvious examples of varying attitudes toward education — varying compared to the norms of the United States and the United Kingdom — that have been successful in terms of standards of living and GNP. Both countries surpass the U.S. and British standards of living, yet each has different approaches to education and work-force training.

Based on its long tradition of apprenticeship, in Germany workers expect and receive considerable ongoing training throughout their careers, most paid for by the government and their employers.

In Japan, the country's rigorous secondary school system produces graduates with what some estimate is the equivalent of a U.S. four-year college education. This explains why large Japanese companies expect new employees, just out of high school, to be capable of immediately completing an engineering course of study before assuming their places on the factory floors.[12]

Other European and Asian countries have developed similar systems, and most are now integrating continuing education into their work-force training programs.

As industrialized nations transform into knowledge-based economies and developing countries assume the role of main-line manufacturing, higher education institutions worldwide must make comparable shifts in the way they deliver their educational products. It is a difficult transition that must simultaneously address technology adaptation and confront deeply entrenched percep-tions on more traditional campuses.

---

[1]UNESCO, *World Education Report* (Paris, 1995), 106–107.

[2]Ibid.

[3]For detailed discussions of the importance of lifelong learning to the U.S.'s economy, see James Botkin et al., *Global Stakes: The Future of High Technology in America* (Cambridge, Mass.: Ballinger Publishing Company,

1982); William B. Johnston and Arnold H. Packer, *Workforce 2000: Work and Workers for the Twenty-first Century* (Indianapolis, Ind.: Hudson Institute, 1987), xxvi-xxvii and 95-103; Jack E. Bowsher, *Educating America: Lessons Learned in the Nation's Corporations* (New York: John Wiley & Sons, Inc., 1989), 208-220; and *A Nation at Risk: The Full Account* (Cambridge, Mass.: USA Research, for The National Commission on Excellence in Education, 1984).

[4]International Bank for Reconstruction and Development, *Higher Education: The Lessons of Experience* (Washington, D.C., 1994).

[5]"A Survey of Education," *The Economist*, 28 November 1992.

[6]International Bank, *Higher Education*, 33.

[7]Ibid., 16–19.

[8]Ibid., 34.

[9]"Survey of Education," *Economist*, 7.

[10]For an analysis of the changing ratio of older students to traditional students and of the effects of the change, see Arthur Lewvine and Associates, *Shaping Higher Education's Future: Demographic Realities and Opportunities, 1990–2000* (San Francisco, Jossey-Bass Publishers, 1989), and current issues of *The Chronicle of Higher Education* (weekly, 1255 23rd St., Washington, DC 20037).

[11]Ken Dychtwald and Joe Flower, *Age Wave: The Challenges and Opportunities of an Aging America* (Los Angeles: Jeremy P. Tarcher, Inc., 1989), 3.

[12]Ray Marshall and Marc Tucker, *Thinking for a Living: Education and the Wealth of Nations* (New York: Basic Books, a division of HarperCollins Publishers, Inc., 1992), 44, 49.

The price tag for a four-year undergraduate degree can now run as high as $100,000.

—William E. Simon,
   Former Secretary of the Treasury and
   President, John M. Olin Foundation,
   in *The Wall Street Journal*

2

THE COSTS/BENEFITS EQUATION

It is not an overstatement to say that a college education is becoming what it was 100 years ago: prohibitively expensive to all but the world's most well off.

U.S. HIGHER EDUCATION MEETS THE BOTTOM LINE

Higher education in the United States alone is an increasingly troubled $213 billion industry.[1] Other countries' higher education systems also face severe budget constraints.

I offer this focused look at the U.S. education dilemma because it is a bellwether for the world's other education markets and, if solutions emerge, can offer a paradigm for change.

Perhaps the most pressing concern regarding higher education is the astounding increase in the costs of attending college. While the 1980s saw health-care costs rise a whopping 117%, the price of an education at a private college jumped 146%, and the average cost of attending a public college increased by a nearly as impressive 109%.[2]

17

Today, annual tuition and fees at public four-year institutions equal 9% of the median American family income; attending a private institution requires 38% of the median family income.[3] College costs continue to outdistance inflation, and their rapid increase effectively denies educational opportunity to those unable to afford the escalating expense.

These statistics represent a national crisis: Education is one of the few industries in the United States that is becoming less rather than more productive. This is not a minor issue, because higher education employs some 2 million people, a third of them faculty members, and annually enrolls nearly 14 million students. Thus about 5% of the U.S. population either works or studies within the higher education structure.

Part of the problem with costs relates to the expansion and upgrading undertaken by U.S. colleges and universities in the past two decades. These were necessary in order to meet the growing enrollment of baby boom students and to remain academically competitive.

In its quest for quality the higher education system has invested in advanced technology and costly physical plants that often sit unused for four or five months each year. This problem will worsen as empty residence halls, no longer filled with traditional college-age students, continue to incur maintenance costs.

At the same time access to higher education for geographically distant students, those who must travel, and others who cannot attend campus-held classes is becoming a high priority. As Americans recognize the importance of a college education to their careers, to their quality of life, to their economy, and to their children's futures, they are increasingly concerned about universal access to higher education. In an increasingly competitive world economy, the United States cannot let people with potential drop out of the education system. If, indeed, they do, they also drop out of the economic system — at ever-more unpalatable costs to society. This point is dramatically made by Johnston and Packer in *Workforce 2000* in their prediction that:

> During the 1985–2000 period, the good fortune to be born in or to immigrate to the United States will make less difference than the luck or initiative to be well-educated and well-trained. For individuals, the good jobs of the future will belong to those who have skills that enable them to be productive in a high-skill, service economy. For the nation, the success with which the workforce is prepared for high-skilled jobs will be an essential ingredient in maintaining a high-productivity, high-wage economy.[4]

UNIVERSITY TEACHER SHORTAGES

Another change affecting higher education is the teacher shortage predicted to last at least through 2010. In *Prospects for Faculty in the Arts and Sciences,*[5] co-authors William Bowen and Julie Ann Sosa confirm what educators have suspected for several years: By the late 1990s, a substantially increasing rate of enrollment in higher education will result in major shortages of faculty members at colleges throughout the United States. Similar shortages are expected in other countries, where college enrollments already strain the capacities of campuses to deliver in-person instruction.

As the children of the 77 million baby boomers move through U.S. colleges and universities, they will expand demand for faculty at the same time that many professors, hired to meet the baby boom demand of the 1960s and 1970s, are scheduled to retire. Unless a means is found to deliver education to more students without radically increasing the number of faculty, many would-be students will be closed out of the higher education system.

WORKER RETRAINING: AN INTERNATIONAL MARKET

Business and labor leaders recognize the importance of retraining workers with skills that meet 21st century employment needs.[6]

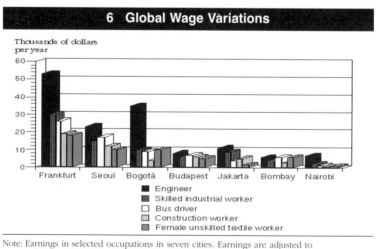

6 Global Wage Variations

Thousands of dollars per year

Frankfurt   Seoul   Bogotá   Budapest   Jakarta   Bombay   Nairobi

■ Engineer
▦ Skilled industrial worker
☐ Bus driver
▥ Construction worker
▨ Female unskilled textile worker

Note: Earnings in selected occupations in seven cities. Earnings are adjusted to reflect purchasing power parity. Data are for 1994.
Source: Union Bank of Switzerland 1994.

The education imperative for workers applies to both industrialized and developing countries and their workers. In *Workers in an Integrating World*, a 1995 report by the World Bank, in virtually every country, more highly educated workers *who are employed* make the most money.[7] However, the World Bank also found that in some developing countries such as India, Bangladesh, and Mexico there are many over-educated workers and too few job opportunities because high illiteracy rates elsewhere in their societies are a drag on their economies.

There is now a consensus that nearly 50% of U.S. workers are employed in some aspect of the "knowledge," or "information," economy, although the definition of what constitutes "information work" is undergoing continued re-evaluation.[8] Consequently, the United States' competitive edge in what is now a global marketplace is based on its ability to teach workers not just to be technically proficient, but to think, to evaluate, to adapt, to use information resources, and to become lifelong learners. A similar transformation is underway in the European Union countries, Canada, Japan, and Singapore.

These skills are critical in all areas of industry, not just among top-level management.

Economists estimate that as many as 40 million people have been dislocated by the "restructuring" in world manufacturing during the last 15 years. In his *Thriving on Chaos*, Tom Peters noted that "since 1980, the Fortune 500 have shed a staggering

2.8 million jobs."[9] Peters' book was published in 1987. In the 1990s, another 3.1 million people were laid off by corporate America, according to the Chicago-based outplacement firm Challenger, Gray, and Christmas. More restructuring will take place as these companies respond to marketplace demand and further competitive threats.

The changing nature and skill requirements of the U.S. workplace have been comprehensively documented by Johnston and Packer in *Workforce 2000:*

> As the economies of developed nations move further into the post-industrial era, human capital plays an ever-more-important role in their progress. As the society becomes more complex, the amount of education and knowledge needed to make a productive contribution to the economy becomes greater.[10]

Later in their analysis, Johnston and Packer state:

> The jobs that will be created between 1987 and 2000 will be substantially different from those in existence today. A number of jobs in the least-skilled job classes will disappear, while high-skilled professions will grow rapidly. Overall, the skill mix of the economy will be moving rapidly upscale, with most new jobs demanding more education and higher levels of language, math and reasoning skills...Among the fastest-growing jobs, the trend toward higher educational requirements is striking. Of all the new jobs that will be created over the 1983-2000 period, more than half will require some education beyond high school, and almost a third will be filled by college graduates. Today, only 22% of all occupations require a college degree.[11]

The changes forecast by Johnston and Packer are occurring throughout the developed, industrialized world among workers seeking better skills and employers wanting more productivity. While countries struggle to define their positions as both trading partners and international competitors, they also are challenged to transform their educational systems to respond to a global economy with shifting and disappearing boundaries.

Clearly, new tools and concepts are required to master this rampant change in our environment. Higher levels of education are imperative for workers in every upward-developing country.

The turbulence of change and the need to adjust are manifest. Yet, for the worker who needs retraining, the military man or woman, the rural adult learner, shift workers, homebound parents, the gifted high school student with no opportunity to take college-level classes at his or her high school, and various others, access to educational opportunities generally and to college coursework and credit specifically has been difficult, if not impossible.

Indeed, as I have noted, at the end of the 20th century, higher education may be close to becoming the privilege it was at the century's beginning. It need not be, however. Higher education for the smallest number would be a tragic legacy for us to leave succeeding generations required to compete in the global economy of the 21st century.

ELEMENTARY AND SECONDARY EDUCATION

The United States' elementary and secondary schools have also had to grapple with shifting circumstances. U.S. schools have attempted to meet two important goals: enriching the classroom experience and providing access to education to a wide and varied population. In addition, these two issues, frequently referred to as "excellence and equity," have been accompanied by a host of other considerations.

State-mandated changes. New, state-mandated changes in curriculum call for more breadth and depth in courses that schools, particularly at the secondary level, are required to offer. These reforms affect schools of every town, city, county, and school district in America.

Requirements for high school graduation have been radically upgraded in many states, with special emphasis placed on mathematics, science, and languages. State colleges and universities across the country also are emphasizing the importance of these subjects by elevating admission requirements in these areas. Unfortunately, the task of meeting requirements at both the secondary and college levels is aggravated by a shortage of appropriate teachers and by budgetary pressures.

In addition to the curricular changes called for, most states now require teachers to participate in professional development or in-service training courses on a regular basis. The importance of professional development cannot be underestimated: To keep pace with the expanding educational requirements of their students, teachers must stay current with the most recent advances in their fields. Yet, for many teachers such courses are unavailable, inaccessible, or at best inconvenient.

Teacher shortages and budget constraints. As noted in *Linking for Learning*, the report on distance education issued in 1989 by the U.S. Department of Commerce's Office of Technology Assessment,

> Shifting economic and demographic patterns have left many small and rural schools with declining student populations and even more limited financial and instructional resources. ... Solutions such as school consolidation or transporting students or teachers have often been stretched to their geographic limits; these approaches are also disruptive and politically unpopular.[12]

Yet these schools must provide the basics of a good education and, if possible, broaden their students' intellectual exposure beyond the confines of their immediate locales.

Struggling to provide a basic education to all students, many schools have few remaining resources with which to meet the unique needs of individuals who either have difficulty learning or are intellectually gifted. This is especially true for schools located in areas that are culturally isolated, economically disadvantaged, or both.

When resources must be stretched just to address the needs of the majority of students, there is a painful recognition that gifted students, some of whom perhaps have the potential to provide signature insights about our world and its problems, may go unchallenged. This is a painful situation because, unless such students are challenged early, their ability to see unique relationships and to optimize their conceptualizing skills may be lost forever.

Teacher shortages are yet another area of concern. The current shortage of qualified teachers in three key areas — math, science, and languages — is projected to worsen dramatically over the next two decades. For lack of a better alternative, some secondary schools have resorted to hiring teachers to teach subjects for which they are less than fully prepared. Finding teachers qualified to teach English as a second language is particularly critical in many locations.

This problem is shared by both rural and urban schools. Often schools cannot afford the luxury of hiring teachers for courses such as trigonometry or Latin if only a few students will enroll. And some schools cannot convince subject-qualified teachers to relocate to their geographic area.

The ongoing dilemma of whether to focus financial and teaching resources on breadth or depth in the curriculum presents yet another problem for the world's schools. Struggling with budget and personnel constraints, many schools must choose between curriculum that covers a large number of subjects lightly or an intensive, highly focused curriculum that covers key subjects in depth but other areas only superficially, if at all.

This dilemma cuts to the heart of the curriculum reform debate: Will a broad-based, general education or a more focused education (for example, a concentration on math and science) better prepare students for the world they will face as adults?

Although proponents for both sides of the debate have presented compelling rationales over the past several years, most educators still believe the goal is to find a way to offer both breadth and depth, ensuring the most comprehensive educational grounding possible.

INTERNATIONAL PROBLEMS, LOCAL SOLUTIONS

The United States is not alone in its drive for elementary and secondary school reform, but the educational philosophies differ considerably in other countries. As *The Economist* noted in its 1992 report on world education, education reform has become an international preoccupation:

> The most comprehensive reform programme has been the one implemented by the British government since 1988. This is a mixture of centralization (imposing a national curriculum and reducing the role of local education authorities) and competition (giving schools an incentive to compete for pupils and encouraging pupils to compete for results). This has attracted many imitators and would-be imitators. Sweden is reorganizing its school system into an internal market. Denmark has introduced per-capita funding for technical colleges. Singapore is going for league tables [published competitive rankings] to stimulate competition between schools. American reformers would like to introduce vouchers and national tests. Other reformers are doing just the opposite. In South Korea and Japan the education ministries want to delegate power to local government. The Japanese authorities strongly disapprove of league tables of schools.[13]

Not only is this global concern with reform necessary at all levels of education, it offers a payoff to those on the receiving end, both young students and adult learners.

If virtue gets its reward in heaven, education gets its payoff on payday. Learning power is earning power. How to make education affordable and accessible is our next challenge.

[1]Chester E. Finn and Bruno V. Manno, "What's Wrong With the American University," *Wilson Quarterly* 20, No. 1 (Winter 1996): 44–45.

[2]Ibid.

[3]Ibid.

[4]William B. Johnston and Arnold H. Packer, *Workforce 2000: Work and Workers for the Twenty-first Century* (Indianapolis, Ind.: Hudson Institute, 1987), 103.

[5]William Bowen and Julie Ann Sosa, *Prospects for Faculty in the Arts and Sciences* (Princeton, N.J.: Princeton University Press, 1989).

[6]See David T. Kearns and Dennis P. Doyle, *Winning the Brain Race: A Bold Plan to Make Our Schools Competitive* (San Francisco: ICS Press, 1988), 1–14; Jack E. Bowsher, *Education America: Lessons Learned in the Nation's Corporations* (New York: John Wiley & Sons, Inc., 1989), 13–44; and Marvin Cetron and Thomas O'Toole, *Encounters With the Future: A Forecast of Life Into the 21st Century* (New York: McGraw-Hill, 1982), 253–271. Note also the statement by United Auto Workers economist Daniel Laria: "Resisting automation is probably a lower route to employment than accepting it." (Ibid., 267).

[7]World Development Bank, *World Education Report 1995* (Washington, D.C., 1995), 39.

[8]Wilson P. Dizard, Jr., *The Coming Knowledge Age: An Overview of Technology, Economics, and Politics, Third Edition* (New York: Longman Inc., 1989), 97–105.

[9]Tom Peters, *Thriving on Chaos: Handbook for a Management Revolution* (New York: Harper & Row, 1987), 5.

[10]Johnston and Packer, *Workforce 2000*, xxvi–xxvii.

[11]Ibid., 96–97.

[12]United States Congress, Office of Technology Assessment, *Linking for Learning: A New Course for Education*, ITA-SET-430 (Washington, D.C.: U.S. Government Printing Office, November 1989), 27–28.

[13]"A Survey of Education," *The Economist*, 28 November 1992.

Each person should be able to access high quality learning opportunities appropriate to their needs throughout their life. They should be able to do this from home, the work place, local community-based centers, or through educational institutions.

3

—Vision statement: Open Learning Agency, British Columbia, Canada

DISTANCE EDUCATION: THE ROOTS OF CYBERSCHOOLS

Distance education is part of the answer to the quest for affordable, accessible higher education.

Distance education has graduated from its roots in mail-order correspondence courses — in their own day both innovative and democratizing — to become an exciting, effective way to learn. It can employ almost every communications technology application that has arrived in this century, be it a TV course, courseware, on-line instruction, an Internet class, or a virtual campus.

Distance education via electronic instruction won't solve all the world's education delivery problems, but it can help. If developed wisely and with the combined efforts of the public and private sectors throughout the world, distance education will use increasingly available communications technology to bring education to the learner — whether that learner be in the United States or Europe or anywhere on the globe where satellite transmissions, fiber links, televisions, computers, or various combinations forming electronic platforms are available.

THE MEDIUM ISN'T THE MESSAGE

Much of my life has been devoted to the development and deployment of communications tools for the public at large. During that process, I have found that distance education is an instance where the late media philosopher Marshall McLuhan's (http://www.digitallantern.com/McLuhan/) famous maxim, "The medium is the message,"[1] stated in his seminal work, *Understanding Media*, should not be taken literally.

While communications technology often fascinates us, the content it conveys — education, entertainment, news, and the like — was and still is king. Striving for human interaction to understand, interpret, and debate that content just happens to consume most of our lives. McLuhan's later work, *The Medium Is the Massage*,[2] spelled out in more graphic terms how technology can shape our perception of content. This undeniable phenomena is the driving force behind much of the concern and debate over education and technology and is addressed in later chapters.

A BRIEF HISTORY

Historical context is useful in understanding the evolution of distance education from its text-based, correspondence course beginnings to its current foundations in technology.

Early examples of distance education are generally attributed to the late 19th century, when formal correspondence courses were developed. But the first distance learner to receive full university credit probably did so in the 18th century, when a home-bound student on a remote agricultural estate made informal arrangements with a university lecturer to receive course notes and text books by mail and completed examinations in writing. The lecturer likely pocketed an "incentive" fee from the student, and university officials were never aware the student on the class roll was a phantom.

As social, demographic, and economic changes shaped both 19th and 20th centuries, some leaders in education worked to fashion new ways to bring education to those who wanted it. The single most outstanding higher education advancement in 19th century America was U.S. President Abraham Lincoln's signing in 1862 of the Morrill Act, which initiated development of a system of state-supported universities that was intended to make college education more affordable and available to U.S. citizens. The act provided a 19th century bricks-and-mortar solution to the education distribution dilemma in one part of the world. The 1887 Hatch Act established agricultural experiment stations, followed in 1914 by the Smith-Lever Act, which authorized county extension agents for agriculture and home economics. These were some of the first attempts to take education directly from state universities to adult learners in the United States.

Today, arguably, the most successful efforts to bring higher education to more people at affordable costs involve distance education.

Initially, telecourses, or televised instruction, proved to be one of the most promising of the technology-based distance education alternatives. Advances in communications technologies such as cable television, fiber optics, microwave, slow-scan television, satellites, microcomputer networks, fax machines, videocassette recorders (VCRs), and the Internet have allowed telecourse and courseware design and delivery to become even more effective.

Beginning in the mid-1990s, the rapid evolution and adaptation of the Internet with its graphical and interactive World Wide Web provided an immediate distance learning medium that distance teaching institutions have been quick to employ. At this writing, high-speed cable TV modems capable of delivering TV broadcast and Internet services, telephone lines with supercharged ADSL or ISDN service, and satellite transmissions beamed directly to homes with telephone return links are being tested for distance education and will likely be in use by consumers by the time the reader takes this book from the shelf. The technology, I believe, holds the potential to turn every living room on the globe into a real-time, interactive classroom.

WORLDWIDE DISTANCE HIGHER EDUCATION

Education systems in sparsely populated countries such as Australia, Canada, and the Scandinavian countries have employed distance learning programs largely in the form of by-mail correspondence courses for more than 100 years.

Distance education is used effectively in Australian higher education in particular, where seven universities teach at a distance to about 15,000 students, or to around 10% of their total enrollments. In addition there are 29,000 students enrolled in the distance education programs of the Colleges of Advanced Education and 350,000 in the Technical and Further Education sector.

In many countries traditional higher education institutions collaborate to design and deliver distance education. Examples are Federation Interuniversitaire de L'Enseignement à Distance in France, which coordinates distance education centers at 22 universities, and Italy's Consorzio Per L'Universita a Distanz, which designs learning materials and support services for students who register with universities that are members of the consortium. In Ontario, Canada, Contact North serves 27 communities through coordinating centers in member colleges and universities.

There also are stand-alone distance learning institutions in more than 20 countries. Many have huge student enrollments. For example, in Thailand the Sukhothai Thammathirat Open University, established in 1978, has some 200,000 students and a target of admitting around 500,000. Established in the early 1980s and offering more than 500 courses a year, China's Central Radio and Television University is the largest open learning institution in the world. CRTVU has an annual total student enrollment of about 1.5 million students. It offers three-year junior college level programs. Germany's FernUniversität has a student body of around 30,000.[3] Others, in order of their founding, include:

Open University of South Africa (1951)
Universidad Nacional de Educación a Distancia, Spain (1972)
Everyman's University, Israel (1974)
Allama Iqbal Open University, Pakistan (1974)
Universidad Estatal a Distancia, Costa Rica (1977)
Universidad Nacional Abierta, Venezuela (1977)
Anadolu University, Turkey (1981)
Open Universiteit, The Netherlands (1981)
Sri Lanka Institute of Distance Education (1981)
Kyongi Open University, Korea (1982)
University of the Air, Japan (1983)
Universitas Terbuka, Indonesia (1984)
Indira Gandi National Open University, India (1985)
National Open University Taiwan (1987)
Al Quds Open University Jordan (1987)
Universidade Aberta, Portugal (1988)
Open Learning Institute of Hong Kong (1989)

The Confederation of Independent States reportedly has some 14 autonomous distance teaching universities.

But it was the United Kingdom's highly innovative British Open University (BOU), founded in 1969, which quickly became an international distance education model by making college-level learning available to the general public. This institution truly opened the doors to distance learning and defied the "education for the elite" philosophy that still to a certain extent dominates European higher education systems.

Championed by then Prime Minister Harold Wilson, BOU was created as an alternative system for achieving a higher education degree. Its courses blended print, radio, and some video presentations with campus visits. They were designed to appeal to students unable to attend universities full-time or "in residence." There were no admission requirements. Anyone could enroll in BOU, but only if a student successfully completed course requirements could he or she obtain a degree.

To support its far-flung population, BOU established sites throughout the United Kingdom where students could take exams and meet with tutors. Beginning with an enrollment of 40,000 in 1971, BOU now counts more than 150,000 in its student body. The university also has distributed its course materials for use in the United States and, in 1994, counted 5,000 of its students from the European Union. Another 8,000 students take BOU courses through partnership agreements with institutions in Central and Eastern Europe.

One of BOU's largest contributions to distance education is that it helped set the precedent for using radio and television to deliver higher education courses.

TV: EDUCATION DIRECT TO YOUR LIVING ROOM

Telecourses have been part of the United States' educational delivery system since televised classes were first broadcast into America's homes more than 30 years ago. Typically received by ordinary home antennas from local broadcast television stations, these early, rudimentary telecourses brought traditional classroom presentations directly into students' living rooms.

Chicago Citywide College, an extension of the City College of Chicago, took the lead in testing and developing this new education delivery system.[4] Supported by a grant from the Ford Foundation's Fund for the Advancement of Education, Chicago Citywide College began broadcasting telecourses over Chicago's public educational television station, WTTW, in 1956. From those early days of trial-and-error experimentation, Chicago Citywide College has continued its commitment to expand the applicability and enhance the effectiveness of telecourse instruction. And, although many other colleges have since followed its lead, Chicago Citywide's program is generally recognized to have set the stage for educational television today.

Also in 1956, while Chicago Citywide College was establishing itself, another Ford Foundation-supported project for television in higher education was begun at Pennsylvania State University. The purpose of the Penn State project was to explore the potential of closed-circuit television for on-campus instruction. It was successful. The project had produced 28 courses for the university by 1966.

Beyond closed-circuit courses, the 1950s spawned university-owned and -operated television stations. Examples include KUON, at the University of Nebraska-Lincoln, and WUNC, at the University of North Carolina at Chapel Hill. Many have since developed into highly effective statewide networks.

Widespread experimentation with telecourses continued at U.S. universities through the 1960s, 1970s, and 1980s. Educators at Michigan State University, at East Lansing, American University in Washington, D.C., Case Western Reserve University in Cleveland, Ohio, and Iowa State University in Ames, among others, explored the possibilities offered by instructional television. They worked with a variety of professionals — teachers, instructional designers, graphic artists, educational technologists, and students — to find the most effective ways to create and deliver telecourses.

COMMERCIAL TV'S EARLY EDUCATION FORAYS

Colleges and universities that did not own a station or a closed-circuit system got their opportunity to experiment with television courses when the commercial networks became interested in educational television.

WCBS/New York first broadcast New York University's (NYU) Sunrise Semester series on comparative literature in 1957. By 1958, NBC was broadcasting "Atomic Age Physics" on Continental Classroom over 150 network stations across the country. Funded in part by another grant from the Ford Foundation, the physics series received high marks from educators for academic quality and the usefulness of the accompanying support materials for students and local teachers. More than 300 colleges and universities offered "Atomic Age Physics" the first year, and several other courses followed in succeeding years.

Unfortunately, the series required a heavy subsidy, and NBC dropped it after a few seasons. Nevertheless, educators, programmers, and producers learned valuable lessons about telecourses from the experience. Indeed, they learned that a program with high academic standards could be created that would be accepted by teachers and students; that a market for such programs existed; and that, as always, financial issues needed to be considered.

After a 25-year run, NYU's Sunrise Semester was discontinued in 1982.

PUBLIC TELEVISION

Another landmark event for telecourses in the early 1960s was the passing of the Federal Educational Television Facilities Act of 1962. This legislation empowered the federal government to fund the building and equipping of public television stations, thereby extending educational television's broadcast reach.

In response to the growing interest in telecourses, the Great Plains Regional Instructional Library was created in 1963 by an agency of the KUON-TV/Nebraska ETV Network in affiliation with the University of Nebraska-Lincoln. The library's goal was to serve as a clearing house that would acquire, maintain, and lend to schools those programs and series that had continuing educational value.

Headquartered in Lincoln, Neb., the library now houses some 2,300 educational programs for elementary, secondary, and higher education and produces the young reader "Reading Rainbow" series for the Public Broadcasting System.

WATERSHED: THE PUBLIC BROADCASTING ACT OF 1967

Probably the biggest attempt to advance educational television in the United States occurred with the passage of the Public Broadcasting Act of 1967. It recognized the potential of broadcast television to inform and enlighten — as well as entertain — the public.

This legislation authorized the creation of the Corporation for Public Broadcasting (CPB), which was charged with the "responsibility of assisting new stations in getting on the air, establishing one or more systems of interconnection, obtaining grants from federal and other sources, providing funds to support local programming and conducting research and training projects."[5]

The Corporation for Public Broadcasting was not a production or networking facility. The Public Broadcasting System (PBS) was created in 1969 to serve as CPB's television network. Its functions were to select, schedule, and distribute programming for the widespread system of PBS-affiliated stations. Through that network, a nationwide system of public television comprised of some 350 local stations came into being.

The question from an education standpoint, is could much of this development have been accomplished more efficiently by outsourcing more of it to the private sector? As an entrepreneur with decades of experience in this field, I think the answer is, was, and will continue to be *yes*. My rationale for this is explained in greater depth in Chapter 10.

COMMUNITY COLLEGE TV

In the mid-1970s, community colleges began producing their own telecourse series and related support materials to attract broader audiences and extend the reach of their campuses. Miami-Dade Community College in Miami, Fla., Coastline Community College District in Fountain Valley, Calif., and Dallas County Community College in Dallas, Texas, were three of the colleges most active in this field. Since then, many community colleges have joined together in regional consortiums that currently produce some of the best telecourse programs available throughout the world.

ANNENBERG/CPB AND THE STAR SCHOOLS PROGRAM

The 1980s produced an explosion of alternative instructional delivery systems for public elementary, secondary, and higher education in America. Fueling major research and experimentation during this period was former Ambassador to Great Britain Walter Annenberg's establishment in 1981 of the landmark Annenberg/CPB Project, through which the Annenberg School of Communications at the University of Pennsylvania contracted to provide $10 million a year for 15 years to CPB.

The goal of the project was to expand opportunities for people to acquire a quality college education at an affordable cost. To that end, the project supported the development of a collection of telecourses that could be offered to students at more convenient times and places than the traditional classroom hours. It also funded demonstrations of new applications of the telecommunication and information technologies in higher education. The purpose of this funding was to explore improvements in education made possible by advances in technology.[6]

Recently, the federal government has taken a more active role in exploring — and funding — distance education. Perhaps the most ambitious undertaking so far is the federal government's Star Schools Program for elementary and secondary schools. Created by the Omnibus Trade Bill and Competitive Act in 1988, the Star Schools Program was designed to address "critical needs in the rebuilding of our education system to meet domestic and international challenges."

The priorities of the Star Schools Program were "to create multistate, organizationally diverse partnerships to write and deliver both core and enrichment curriculum, and to create opportunities for disadvantaged students to receive remote instruction."[7] By insisting on multistate, multi-institutional partnerships, the bill's authors hoped to encourage new ways for the nation's remotely located and under-served students to gain access to quality education. Distance education technology has been the central vehicle for achieving this goal.

41

The Star Schools Program was authorized as a five-year program with an overall funding limit of $100 million. In pursuit of this goal, Congress appropriated $33.5 million over a two-year period to ensure United States students "access to basic and advanced courses in mathematics, science, and foreign languages."[8]

Four projects were selected for the first two-year grant period, three satellite-delivered projects and one based on a combination of computers and telecommunications. At this writing, Star Schools' prospects for continued federal funding are good.

However, programs so critically important to students in the knowledge age should not have to live or die depending upon the vagaries of Congressional funding priorities. I believe Star Schools should try to find a way to stand on its own. Indeed, with shrinking government coffers, most publicly funded entities should be creating alternative, private-sector survival plans — it's an exercise in self-sustainability. History indicates that often when public funding ends, so does the project.

As we enter the 21st century, our challenge will be to build upon the insights and experiences gained in the past four decades. These advances have created unprecedented opportunities to tailor education to the needs of the students, rather than having students structure their education around the needs of institutions.

With broad-scale ability to become educated comes broad-scale opportunity — economic and otherwise. With recognizable opportunity and broad-scale access to it comes a broad-scale sense of fairness and hope. I believe a sense of fairness and a hopeful attitude are positive elements. Our world society needs them. They are confidence-builders personally, organizationally, nationally, and globally.

[1]Marshall McLuhan, *Understanding Media: The Extensions of Man* (New York: New American Library, 1964), 23.

[2]Marshall McLuhan and Quentin Fiore, *The Medium Is the Massage: An Inventory of Effects* (New York: Bantam Books, 1967), 26.

[3]Barbara L. Watkins and Stephen J. Wright, *The Foundation of American Distance Education: A Century of Collegiate Correspondence Study* (Dubuque, Iowa: Kendall/Hunt Publishing Company, 1991), 199, 295, 297.

[4]Michael G. Moore and Melody M. Thompson, *The Effects of Distance Learning: A Summary of Literature* (University Park, Pa.: The American Center for the Study of Distance Education, 1990), 3.

[5]D. N. Wood and D. G. Wylie, "Reaching New Students Through New Technologies," *Educational Telecommunications* (Belmont, Calif.: Wadsworth Publishing Company, 1977), 33.

[6]Annenberg/CPB project statement, 1987.

[7]United States Congress, Office of Technology Assessment, *Linking for Learning: A New Course for Education*, ITA-SET-430 (Washington, D.C.: U.S. Government Printing Office, November 1989), 136.

[8]U.S. Senate Committee on Labor and Human Resources, *The Star Schools Program Assistance Act of 1987*, 100th Cong., 1st sess., 1987, S. Rept. 100-44, 1.

The Virtual Classroom is one of those things that is best experienced, like a sunset swim in ocean waves, in order to fully understand it.

—Starr Roxanne Hiltz,
  in *The Virtual Classroom*

THE VIRTUAL CLASSROOM OF THE 21ST CENTURY

The days when the overhead projector was the highest-tech teaching tool to grace the halls of ivy are over. The numbers prove it. For example, in 1994 e-mail was used in only 8% of college courses in the United States. By 1995, that percentage had almost tripled — to 21 percent. In 1994, only 4% of college courses were taught using multimedia. In 1995, the percentage had doubled. A modest beginning, but, as Kenneth Green, director of the U.S. Annual Campus Computing Survey, wrote in the March/April 1996 issue of *Change* magazine, "Most colleges and universities have finally passed the point of critical mass affecting the instructional use of information technology."

Technology doesn't necessarily have to come in the form of a microcomputer. For technophobic teachers, perhaps just an Internet access device would suffice. But the higher education establishment must adapt to technology in the lecture hall — or perhaps even get used to technology *as* the lecture hall. A true paradigm shift needs to occur in the way college educators and the higher education establishment perceive and design the education environment.

Equally important, technology can be used to create a less expensive way to deliver higher education to those who want it. While there will never be a substitute for the ivy-covered experience of the college campus, advances in computers, cable television, and satellites and the ubiquitousness of the Internet and its World Wide Web should and will make higher education available to the most people at the lowest cost — worldwide.

THE LIVING ROOM AS CLASSROOM

The idea is to deliver education to people, instead of people to education. The idea is to deliver education to the living room — whether that living room be in Alabama or Argentina. Why now? Because, as we all know, earning a living in post-industrial, knowledge age society will require lifelong learning, training, and retraining at every level. For the vast majority, interrupting work life to study in a traditional university setting is out of the question.

I predict that the dawning of the 21st century will reveal that we already have ushered in the full use of technology-based institutions that can function side-by-side with traditional universities.

In technospeak, these new education-providing mechanisms are called "virtual." What does virtual mean? The term virtual is used in computer science to refer to something whose existence is simulated with software, rather than actually existing in some physical form.

The virtual university is education dispensed from an electronic platform, instead of a lecture hall podium. Indeed, work on virtual classrooms and virtual universities has been taking place since the 1980s, both in the private sector and in the public sector at university consortia, governors' conferences, and public television studios.

For example, Apple Computer, Inc. is creating a software/hardware/network package called the Apple Virtual Campus.[1] It uses the Macintosh computer as its foundation technology and promises speech, videoconferencing, and telephone service all from a learner's desktop. The software part of the package, called Apple Open Collaboration Environment, allows simultaneous communications anytime, anywhere. The whole idea is to allow students, faculty, and administrators at a university to be able to record, send, and receive information and messages from any location to any other location at any moment in time.

At Sun Microsystems, engineers have created a virtual classroom package that allows nine to 12 students in any location in the world to attend class together live from the desktop, through video and audio cards in their computers.

The world-renowned British Open University in the United Kingdom is developing a new program called Stadium using Sun's Java Internet software, which is designed to allow thousands of students at a time to listen and participate in special guest lectures given on the university's virtual campus.

Stadium's creators tout it as an experiment in "very large telepresence." Telepresence captures the mood of an event — applause, laughter, shouting, whispers between neighbors, and the like — using software. As this book is being written, Stadium is in the prototype development stage. The software engineers at BOU's Knowledge Media Institute are hoping Stadium will host an event with 100,000 participants by the end of 1996.

Virtual Classrooms: Better Than Real?

Agreed, for the uninitiated the concept is a little tough to grasp. But, as virtual classroom design innovator Starr Roxanne Hiltz, head of the Computer Assisted Learning Program at the New Jersey Institute of Technology, advises,

> The virtual classroom is one of those things that is best experienced, like a sunset swim in ocean waves, in order to fully understand it…think of all the different kinds of learning tools and spaces and ritualized forms of interaction that take place within a traditional classroom, and within an entire college campus or high school. All of these things exist within a virtual classroom, too, except that all of the activities and interactions are mediated by computer software, rather than by face-to-face interaction.[2]

First introduced in the mid-1980s, Hiltz's technology was used by the ConnectEd, or Connected Education, program, part of the New School for Social Research in New York City, to connect instructors in North America with students in Asia, Europe, and Latin America.[3] The technology was used much like the

Internet is used today: A student in Asia could dial a local telephone number to connect to the mainframe computer in New Jersey to receive any course material stored there, to leave or receive papers, or to communicate with an instructor or other class members.

Another way to think about the virtual classroom is to compare it with how interaction takes place in a traditional classroom. In traditional classrooms, most interaction takes place via speaking, listening, reading, and writing. In the virtual classroom, interaction takes place entirely by typing and reading from a computer terminal. If that seems like a less than superior alternative to the traditional classroom, it's really not. Hiltz contends a collaborative learning environment that is computer mediated can support some activities that are difficult or impossible to conduct in face-to-face environments, particularly if there is a large class. In the virtual classroom, discussion and communication about the course become a continuous activity. If a student has an idea or a question, it can be communicated while it is fresh.

The advantages of the virtual university's being virtually anywhere — in a living room, a kitchen corner, or the local library — are obvious, but I'll list them anyway: All students in a particular class don't have to be at the same place at the same time, week after week, for the course of a semester; and the virtual university is open 24 hours a day, seven days a week. For adult learners, with jobs and family responsibilities, the ability to do coursework on their own schedules may make the difference between successfully completing a degree program and dropping out.

If you think about using traditional terms, in the virtual university there are interaction "spaces" created within a software package that are used as so-called classrooms, where teachers lecture and where group discussions take place; there is a communication structure like office hours, where student and teacher can communicate privately. The software also has the ability to administer, collect, and grade tests or assignments and the ability to divide a larger class into smaller working or peer groups for collaborative assignments.[4]

All this can happen within a computer-mediated communication system. Two examples are the local area network, where students and teachers can communicate via electronic bulletin boards, e-mail, and private news groups on the Internet, also called listservs. The local area network by its nature can restrict the virtual classroom to a certain defined area, like a college campus, and a course delivered over the Internet's World Wide Web can have a similar structure and password restrictions.

The concept has been tested and is successful. Currently more than 80 programs worldwide are known to be offering courses partly or completely via computer.

VIRTUAL EDUCATION VISIONS

One of the latest virtual education visions comes from the governors of several of the western U.S states. They intend to create an institution in cyberspace called Western Governors' University. The governors first discussed their virtual university idea at the Western Governors' Association's annual meeting in June 1995 in Park City, Utah. Money, as often is the case in both government and the private sector, was the driver. The concept grew out of a discussion about how to contain the costs of producing expensive distance learning courses and the states' limited capacity to fund increasingly high-cost traditional higher education. What evolved is a vision for a combination of technology and face-to-face modes — specifically cable television, Internet-based courses and summer seminars — delivering education to far flung students in all the idyllic nooks and crannies of this sparsely populated region.

The governors' objectives mirror those of many distance learning programs already in existence. Their goals are similar, too, in that they mention extending educational opportunities to more citizens, reducing the costs of higher education, and shifting the focus of education away from "seat time" and toward competence.[5]

I have one more goal (one which the tenor of the governors' proposal clearly embraces) and that is to truly make the student the focus of the process, not the institution or the teacher.

The governors claim their virtual university is an alternative concept for U.S. higher education, with learning delivered to students on campus, at home, in libraries, or at work. We know the concept works because models have been developed, and it has already been done. In the United States alone National Technological University, Coastline Community College, and over 30 other U.S. universities and colleges have a wealth of experience in delivering electronic, accredited courses that can be referred to for guidance and expertise.

THE VIRTUAL LIBRARY

We have known since the beginnings of civilization that knowledge is power. Dating back to the end of the Middle Ages, at the heart of every traditional university has been a great library. Indeed, in the early 17th century, Sir Francis Bacon may have created one of the first library cataloguing systems. As part of his essay, *In Advancement of Learning*, he divided "all knowledge" according to the faculties of memory, imagination, and reason — complete with subdivisions. In the knowledge age, we can take the great library vision further: At the heart of the great virtual university is a great virtual library. There is enough digital and digitized information being created today to begin to develop virtual libraries filled with the world's knowledge and available to anyone with access to a computer and a modem. Think about it: On-line access to the globe's important information by every scholar in the world.

Here are a few examples: The University of California at Berkeley's Digital Library Project is creating the California Environment Project, which will consist of digitized versions of technical reports, computers models, county general plans, aerial and ground photographs, maps, videos, and other elements of a vast database. Meanwhile, the University of California at Santa Barbara is working on the Alexandria Digital Library, which ultimately will create full-content search-and-retrieval video libraries; and the University of Illinois is building a large-scale digital library testbed with the goal of bringing professional quality search-and-display to Internet information services. The University of Michigan and Stanford University also are working on digital libraries.

All these projects are aiming toward something entirely new: the management of digital as well as digitized information. As Paul Evan Peters, executive director of the Coalition of Networked Information describes it,

> The knowledge objects enabled by this emergent class of digital libraries will be much more like "experience" than they will be like things, much more like programs than documents, and readers will have unique experiences with these objects in an even more profound way than is already the case with books, periodicals, etc.[6]

This is the virtual library of the future. Governments the world over would do well to fund the creation of new digitized and digital content and leave the building of telecommunications infrastructure to deliver it to users to the private sector.

JONES' VIRTUAL LIBRARY IN CYBERSPACE

Using the digitized information resources available today from the U.S. Library of Congress and the National Library of Canada, we at Jones International have created a virtual library in cyberspace: the Global Electronic Library (http://www.jec.edu/knonline/glp/gel.html). This virtual collection, accessible via the Internet's World Wide Web, intends to highlight the best of the digitized library resources around the world. You could say it serves as a "cybrarian" for the students of the virtual university and the knowledge age. Plans are in the works at the Global Electronic Library for the development of a curriculum home page. The page would allow teachers to explore and download lesson plans developed for use with this virtual library's contents for their classes.

The Global Electronic Library currently holds portions of the Library of Congress' American Memory Collection and selected archival information from the Canadian national library. Right now, the Global Electronic Library contains six photographic collections from the American Memory Collection, one recorded sound collection, five text-based collections, and a trio of early motion picture collections.

All have been prepared for Internet access and all are rich primary resources — the kinds of things your local public library once only dreamed about obtaining. They include digitized copies of documents from the Continental Congress of the United States and the Constitutional Convention, circa 1774 to 1790. They also include digitized versions of 351 rare African American pamphlets from the Daniel A. P. Murray collection which offer insights into the attitudes and the ideals of African Americans between the end of the Civil War and World War I.

Also available with a few clicks of a mouse are digitizations of famed Civil War photographer Matthew Brady's daguerreotypes, and life history manuscripts from the Folklore Project of the Depression-era Works Progress Administration.

Soon there will be more digitized resources available. The Library of Congress' National Digital Library project (http://rs6.loc.gov/amhome.html), under the outstanding leadership of its librarian, James Billington, plans to digitize some 5 million items over the next three years. This is the largest repository of information in the world. Congress has allocated $3 million a year for the next five years for the project. Congress also has requested The Library of Congress to raise $3 of private funding for every dollar of public funding for the project. To that end, corporate and individual contributions have come from John Kluge, the David and Lucile Packard Foundation, the W. W. Kellogg Foundation, Ameritech, Bell Atlantic Corporation, the McCormick Tribune Foundation, The Discovery Channel, Eastman Kodak Company, Reuters, Compaq Computer Corporation, The Hearst Foundation, R.R. Donnelly & Sons, NYNEX Corporation, and Nortel. Total funding as of mid-1996 for the project is $32.6 million.

Canadian and the U.K. Collections

The National Library of Canada's contribution to the Global Electronic Library tracks the birth of the Canadian Confederation in 1867 and the influence of the U.S. Civil War on its creation (http://www.nlc-bnc.ca/confed/e-1867.htm). Virtual library patrons have the opportunity to learn that during those years Canada not only feared annexation by the United States, but was a haven for sympathizers from both Northern and Southern states.

In the United Kingdom, a massive effort called the Electronic Libraries Programme has been undertaken by a consortium of universities with $15 million in funding. U.K. universities are digitizing vast collections of 18th and 19th century journals such as *Gentleman's Magazine, The Annual Registry, Philosophical Transactions of the Royal Society,* and many more. Anyone with access to the Internet will be able to peruse them on their desktops. Also being digitized are journals in design and applied arts. While CD-ROM may be the best method of delivery for these journals, interface with the Internet is being explored.

The U.K. program also is exploring on-demand publishing — a way to deliver electronically stored materials to more students at a time. Investigators are interested in developing flexible licensing arrangements for multiple sets of copyrighted materials to be printed and handed out for student use.

Copyright laws are a sticky issue in the world of digitization and virtual electronic libraries. Currently, documents not considered to be in what is called the public domain are subject to copyright laws. Libraries and other institutions that want to put copyrighted material on the World Wide Web or other electronic bulletin board systems still must get permission from the materials' authors or their estates. Music is a particular problem because so many different entities — writers, record companies, publishers — all have rights to the material.

In addition to the electronic library efforts ongoing in the United Kingdom, France is completing its Bibliothéque de la France, which will replace its Bibliothéque Nationale. In conjunction with the building project, the library's aim is to digitize many of its collections. These projects in the United States, United Kingdom, and France are but three of many similar efforts beginning to take shape worldwide.

ANOTHER ON-LINE OPTION

For students who can't wait for all the world's knowledge to be recorded in 1s and 0s, a non-digitized worldwide library project is the On-line Computer Library Center, Inc., (OCLC), headquartered near Columbus, Ohio. It is the world's largest bibliographic computer system. By 1996, it was serving more than 22,000 libraries in 63 countries, including the database of Kinki University library in Osaka, Japan. Information does not have to be digitized to be catalogued in this center, but OCLC is beginning a digitization project on the World Wide Web with some of its electronic journal materials (http://www.oclc.org).

It is hoped that as more and more digitized rare, classical literary artifacts become available to living room-based patrons of virtual libraries, educational barriers that divide societies will begin to crumble. I believe we most likely will see these libraries in cyberspace becoming to the 21st century what the fax machine was to the late 20th century. Information disseminated by fax helped change the world's political balance when the Iron Curtain collapsed in the late 1980s. Wouldn't it be wonderful if in the 21st century the ability to share the world's knowledge through virtual libraries and global virtual universities brought the world to the next level of understanding? It can happen.

TEACHERS AS HOLOGRAMS?

Despite the evidence, there are bound to be arguments in traditional education circles that virtual universities and classrooms lack the synergism of the traditional classroom and students will, therefore, learn less. Understandably, professors appearing as holograms is a discomforting idea. I can understand why these entrenched opinions exist, but I urge their proponents to rethink them.

Here's why. In the virtual classroom, it is virtually impossible to be a passive learner. Students nearly always must react or provide some appropriate input in order to continue to the next phase of an assignment. In addition, virtual courses are more often designed to be collaborative efforts among students than are the traditional lecture hall courses we all knew and loved — at least for the sheer anonymity they provided.

Clearly, all mediums of communication have their advantages and disadvantages. But the research really does show there is no significant difference in the student's ability to learn using technology-based education tools. And not just for computer-aided teaching. Long ago research into whether television was an inferior learning tool proved there is no real difference between learning from TV and learning in the traditional classroom.[7] And with 7 million students now working full time in the United States alone,[8] there certainly is a market for virtual universities to tap.

At the beginning of any paradigm shift — and the knowledge age is demanding a paradigm shift in education delivery — there must be explorers. The technology available today plus the current state of the economics of higher education demand we either become adventurers ourselves or provide the opportunity for others to be.

[1]Author unknown, *"Apple America's Higher Education: A Vision Shared,"* April 16, 1996, http://www.education.apple.com/

[2]Starr Roxanne Hiltz, *The Virtual Classroom* (Norwood, N.J.: Ablex Publishing Corporation, 1994), 4.

[3]Parker Rossman, *The Emerging Worldwide Electronic University: Knowledge Age Global Higher Education* (Westport, Conn.: Greenwood Press, 1992), 46–47.

[4]Hiltz, *Virtual Classroom*, 6.

[5]Western Governors' Association, *From Vision to Reality: A Western Virtual University* (Denver, Colo., 1996), 1.

[6]Paul Evan Peters, "Digital Libraries Are Much More Than Digitized Collections," *Educom Review*, July–August 1995.

[7]Hiltz, *Virtual Classroom*, 20.

[8]Robert Moskowitz, "Wired U," *Internet World*, October 1995, 60.

It appears that (television) is at least on the verge of fulfilling the great hope of the 1940s – that each home could be a university center as long as it had a television set and a willing learner.

—Dee Brock,
 Former Director of Adult Learning
 Programming, Public Broadcasting
 System, United States

KNOWLEDGE TV:
AN ENTREPRENEURIAL APPROACH

Dee Brock wrote the words above in 1985, when she was Director of Adult Learning Programming at the Public Broadcasting System (PBS). That was two years before Jones International launched its cable television education programming channel, Mind Extension University (ME/U), which changed its name to Knowledge TV in late 1996.

Now, more than a decade later, Knowledge TV has made the living room a potential university classroom for at least 26 million cable television subscribers and satellite dish owners in the United States, for viewers of cable and satellite television in various Asian countries including Thailand, China, and South Korea, and for the countries in the European Union.

TV'S IMPACT

For distance education, television arguably has been the transforming technology of the 20th century. The opening of the ultra-high frequency spectrum in the 1960s and 1970s — which brought the explosive growth of non-commercial television stations — plus the advent of cable TV brought education programming home, so to speak.

As anyone who had the experience of sitting through an early TV course well knows, at first televised courses were not polished. Indeed, Brock notes, "the camera was just an observer sitting in the front row"[1] of a college classroom. Televised courses often were only broadcast on closed circuit TV or microwave to other classrooms on campus.

Times have changed. If you haven't seen a televised lesson lately, give yourself a treat and watch one. Television now is used as a teaching medium in a way that engages rather than anesthetizes learners. TV courses now are "produced" — taking advantage of the technology's ability to enhance visually and graphically a student's learning experience. Courses now are broadcast worldwide. As an electronic platform executive, I've been privileged to contribute to this transformation from the private sector.

EXTENDING THE HUMAN MIND

It was and is an entrepreneurial vision: Knowledge TV is in the business of extending the human mind. Knowledge TV is a pro-active, entrepreneurial effort to empower the individual through education and in that manner to contribute to the conversion of information into knowledge, understanding, and wisdom.

I believe Knowledge TV also is not only a part of the evolution of cable television but of the evolution of education itself and other electronic platforms. It focuses on an environment where viewers' minds are actively engaged, where vast amounts of information can be delivered inexpensively, and where distance is erased.

In November 1987, Knowledge TV, as its initial phase, began a basic cable television channel designed to meet diverse needs for education, information, and instruction. Equally important in this age of skyrocketing tuition costs, part of Knowledge TV's original mission included reducing the cost of a higher education degree. As the chart on higher education costs later in this chapter shows, Knowledge TV still is making good on its pledge.

Today the network's programming focuses primarily on for-credit, college-level telecourses in science, fine arts, English, mathematics, foreign languages, health care, general business, computing, and the Internet. It's important to note, however, that Knowledge TV's extensive programming isn't available for those only working on college degrees. Its larger audience is the millions who watch it just to empower themselves. Anyone with cable service that provides Knowledge TV's cable channel can tune in and take advantage of well-produced, insightful educational programming from universities all over the United States, and soon the world. It's much like sitting in on a traditional university class for no credit: You view the Knowledge TV program but don't receive college credit unless you meet certain entrance requirements, enroll in the course, and pay your tuition. Societally, as well as individually, this is very productive.

Let's say you want to know how to teach reading to a preschooler. There's a series of programs on Knowledge TV that tells how. If you want to know how the Southern United States developed after World War II — complete with fascinating archival newsreel and television footage — tune in. If you are baffled by the Internet, tune in. There's a course that explains it on Knowledge TV. Want to learn Microsoft Windows? Tune in. In essence, Knowledge TV has two audiences: the millions who are interested in learning as a self-empowerment tool, and the tens of thousands who want higher education degrees and certificates for professional development.

How Knowledge TV Works

Knowledge TV is distributed to learners via satellite, broadcast, cable and the Internet. Its courses are transmitted by satellite, either directly to homes, businesses, libraries and school classrooms or to cable television systems, then by cable into the same locations.

For college-level courses, for-credit students often use a videocassette recorder to tape the class, then replay it at their convenience. This enables them to fit coursework into their own schedules. It also gives them the opportunity to review classes to more fully understand the topics, concepts or the instructor's points. Students who miss a lesson can call the Knowledge TV

Student Support Center, and a representative will send a replacement tape immediately. That way there is as little interruption as possible in the continuity of the course.

Each month, a program schedule listing the course offerings for that period is sent to students and others who have indicated interest in the courseware. (Research indicates that most Knowledge TV students "preview" or watch a course at least once before enrolling in it.) Registered students receive a syllabus that lists the semester's schedule of their courses. In addition, a course catalog indicates what dates a course will be offered and gives a description of the course content, credit, and cost. Courses generally begin in September, January, and May, similar to the schedule a student would expect from the traditional semester structure. At present, Knowledge TV is commencing some semesters on a monthly basis. As the environment becomes more digital, starting semesters daily or even hourly is being considered. Hypothetically, under the new regime a student could register for a course and begin the coursework an hour after he or she enrolled. This new system is, again, designed to be student, rather than teacher or institution, centered. The student's time determines when the course begins.

GETTING STARTED

Students who sign up for college-level courses receive a copy of the *Telecourse Student Survival Handbook* for the appropriate course. The handbook explains administrative procedures, course requirements, assignment and exam procedures, grades, and other relevant information and includes a broadcast schedule with lesson numbers, dates, and times. The purpose of this material is to streamline the administrative process as much as possible so that the student's efforts go into studying and learning rather than into filling out forms and standing in lines.

Students also receive a study guide and a syllabus or letter from the instructor outlining course details and covering information such as assignments and exams. If the course calls for a proctored exam — for example, all of the MBA classes require proctored exams — this information also will be included.

ATTENDANCE

Once the preliminaries are taken care of, students are ready to start "attending class," so to speak, in their homes or offices. While this sounds unstructured, the relative luxury of off-campus learning does not absolve students of good personal study habits. Most Knowledge TV students stress that consistency of personal scheduling is important to maintain the continuity of the course and to stay on top of assignments.

Courses run for a quarter or a semester, similar to on-campus classes. Although students are encouraged to complete the courses within the regular quarter or semester schedule, it is understood that Knowledge TV students may occasionally face personal and professional disruptions to their studies. As a result, course extensions can be arranged if necessary.

SUPPORT

As with any questions about scheduling, classwork, or related concerns, Knowledge TV representatives at the Student Support Center will work with students to help resolve course completion problems. Essentially, the Student Support Center takes the place of on-campus services for both the student and the affiliate university. The center is staffed at Knowledge TV's headquarters in Englewood, Colo. It supports the Knowledge TV-affiliated colleges and universities and the administrative needs of Knowledge TV students. Through the center, Knowledge TV representatives assist students with enrollment, bill them for tuition and fees, mail text-books and support materials, and arrange exams. Center staff also refer students to local schools when appropriate and provide information about transfer of credits. Students also are provided with missed-lesson videotape rentals through the Student Support Center. In addition, Knowledge TV has a student book store and is enlarging its cyberspace student support to include a more elaborate electronic bulletin board system, a listserv, and other electronic support services.

Instructor contact is maintained via telephone, mail, e-mail, and periodic teleconferences with professors to review course topics.

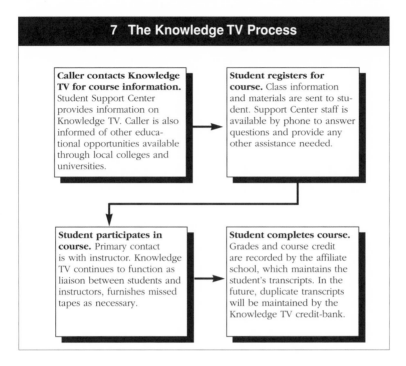

7 The Knowledge TV Process

Caller contacts Knowledge TV for course information. Student Support Center provides information on Knowledge TV. Caller is also informed of other educational opportunities available through local colleges and universities.

Student registers for course. Class information and materials are sent to student. Support Center staff is available by phone to answer questions and provide any other assistance needed.

Student participates in course. Primary contact is with instructor. Knowledge TV continues to function as liaison between students and instructors, furnishes missed tapes as necessary.

Student completes course. Grades and course credit are recorded by the affiliate school, which maintains the student's transcripts. In the future, duplicate transcripts will be maintained by the Knowledge TV credit-bank.

KNOWLEDGE TV'S CONTENT PROVIDERS

Knowledge TV is essentially a public-private partnership. Currently more than 30 affiliate universities, community colleges, and other education providers across the United States broadcast distance learning courses over the channel. Knowledge TV tries to find the best professors and the best university and community college degree programs in the United States to offer its far-flung student base. Students can take part or, in some cases, all of their degree requirements without spending time on campus.

For example, on the community college level, Seattle Central Community College offers an associate of arts degree through

Knowledge TV. Courses are equivalent to freshman and sophomore offerings at four-year institutions and are designed to transfer to four-year bachelor's degree programs. In addition, Colorado Electronic Community College offers the Colorado Community College system's associate of arts degree via Knowledge TV. Colorado community colleges have forged a one-of-a-kind common general education core curriculum that transcends local communities and is completely portable and transferable to many four-year colleges in the United States.

Knowledge TV, although it does deliver various certificates, does not hand out diplomas. A student graduating from the University of Delaware's hotel and restaurant bachelor's degree program via Knowledge TV, for example, will receive his or her degree from the University of Delaware, not Knowledge TV. Knowledge TV is the delivery method. Some courses include printed materials and are only partly delivered by cable television. Others use videotapes and cable or some combination of videotapes, cable, the Internet, and printed materials.

KNOWLEDGE TV's CYBERFAMILY

Two of Jones' most recent creations are on-line campuses developed by Knowledge TV's parent company, Jones Education Company, with help from university and community college professors. They are International University College (http://www.iuc.com) and International Community College. These education institutions don't have physical campuses. They operate electronically with assignments delivered and class discussions conducted via the Internet; the video components are delivered through Knowledge TV. They don't have football teams or dormitories. They do have top-quality courses taught in accelerated format with content provided by some of the finest academic minds at major U.S. universities and community colleges.

IUC, Jones' cyberschool, offers a master's degree program in Business Communications using video cassettes, cable and satellite TV, and the Internet. IUC also has launched a bachelor's degree program in Business Communications and certificates of specialization, much like associate's degrees, in several business and communications-related areas. To date, classes are taught in English. In mid-1996, IUC's students came from 21 states, Canada, Barbados, Antigua, and Germany. Course content has been developed by content experts at such major U.S. universities as Depauw, Michigan State, Purdue, the University of California, the University of Colorado, the University of Denver, the University of Illinois, the University of Oklahoma, and the University of Texas.

In addition, the University of Colorado, Colorado Springs, co-produced with International University College two master's degree programs for students worldwide through Knowledge TV. The Graduate School of Business Administration and the Graduate School of Public Affairs have combined resources to offer the only integrated MBA and MPA program available via electronic technology. The first 18 hours of coursework are the same for both degrees.

International Community College (ICC) is very much what its name implies. It is an institution based in technology where adults from anywhere in the world can take community college-level courses and certificate programs on their own time and on their own schedules. The college is a collaborative effort among the League for Innovation in the Community Colleges — with 80 member community colleges across North America — Jones Education Networks, and Knowledge TV.

ICC premiered in 1996 with its first course offering, "The Emerging Learner." Produced by Dallas Telecourses of the Dallas County Community College District, "The Emerging Learner" is designed to help students become successful distance learners and to equip them with lifelong learning skills readily transferable to the workplace. It's a video series that can be used with all future products developed by the ICC — supporting all students who will be taking courses via telecommunications worldwide.

PAYING FOR A KNOWLEDGE TV EDUCATION

Knowledge TV is a good example of how public-private partnerships can bring the best of both worlds together for the benefit of the consumer — in this case the education consumer. Students can do coursework at Knowledge TV for much less than it would cost for the same on-campus experience. That being said, tuition costs naturally reflect those of its participating schools and fall midway between most public and moderately priced private colleges and universities. But Knowledge TV students pay only for their education, not for school-related transportation, housing, athletic or health fees, or various other costs incurred in living away from home. Plus students can keep their jobs.

Figure 8: Two-Year Colleges 1997-98 Estimated Costs Per Semester (12 Credits)			
Costs	Public	Private	Knowledge TV
Tuition and fees	751	3,428	1,664
Room and board	941	2,272	Existing costs at home
Books and supplies	305	309	459*
Transportation	489	305	Existing costs at home
Other	613	536	Existing costs at home
Total	$ 3,099	$ 6,850	$2,123 (plus costs at home)

Source: The College Board, New York, N.Y.; Jones Education Co.
*Includes video tapes and required course software.

Figure 9: Four-Year Colleges 1997-98 Estimated Costs Per Semester for Undergraduate (12 Credits)			
Costs	Public	Private	Knowledge TV
Tuition and fees	1,556	6,832	2,618
Room and board	2,181	2,775	Existing costs at home
Books and supplies	317	316	571*
Transportation	287	269	Existing costs at home
Other	695	522	Existing costs at home
Total	$5,036	$10,714	$3,189 (plus costs at home)

Source: The College Board, New York, N.Y.; Jones Education Co.
*Includes video tapes and required course software.

Beyond the financial savings is the saving of something equally as precious: time. While the rigors of success in a course are the same, Knowledge TV students don't have to spend time away from their jobs or families as do those who attend classes on campus.

THE NEED

It's clear the need for public-private partnerships such as Knowledge TV, IUC, and ICC has never been greater. Traditional university campuses, be they public or private, cannot make education available to the expanding number of people who need and want it. They don't have the money. And, I would argue, they do not have the entrepreneurial spirit needed to create and implement innovative solutions to education delivery problems worldwide. Those solutions should be addressed immediately and they should be addressed by traditional universities and entrepreneurial private suppliers in concert.

Here are some statistics to ponder:

- There are between 5 million and 7 million part-time higher education students in the United States alone.
- From 1978 to 1993, the number of U.S. 25- to 64-year olds attending school rose 45%.[2]
- One year's tuition at an elite private university or college in the United States costs about $23,000. In 2000 the cost could be as high as $40,000.[3]
- According to the American Society of Training and Development, 65% of all jobs available in the United States

72

and most developed countries in the year 2000 will require some training or education beyond high school, compared with today's 54%.

- By the end of the 20th century, UNESCO, the United Nations Educational, Scientific and Cultural Organization, predicts there could be as many as 1 billion illiterate people in the world. Today there are 900 million.[4]

- More than 100 million students across the globe drop out of school prematurely.[5]

- In China alone some 80 million potential college students await space in the country's filled-to-capacity university system.

Beyond the statistics lies the disturbing trend that most of the world's knowledge is the preserve of the most highly developed countries. Disseminating that knowledge worldwide is imperative if we want a world where peace is the norm, rather than the exception; where business and industry can find the work force to create economic prosperity; and where individuals can have the opportunity to participate in that prosperity.

In addition, the teacher shortage I mentioned in Chapter 2 is not limited to the United States. UNESCO estimates there may be more than 50 million teachers needed worldwide at all education levels by 2000. Payment for their services represents 50% to 80% of current public education expenditures in almost all countries.[6] Adding courses delivered via cable TV or other electronic means to a school's offerings can provide some economies of scale. A conventional course, needing a teacher and a classroom, incurs start-up costs each time it is taught. It is also limited in size. A distance course, once developed and produced, can be distributed at minimal cost to hundreds of thousands of students. Distance education is very cost-effective.

THE PRIMARY AND SECONDARY SCHOOL DILEMMA

In the United States alone, shifting economic and demographic patterns have left small, rural, and inner city primary and secondary schools without resources to teach students the variety of curricula they need to succeed.

Knowledge TV initially attempted to reach those schools with special secondary school curricula through a cooperative agreement with the TI-In Network. TI-In Network was a Texas-based provider of live, interactive television instruction.[7] The attempt was unsuccessful, however, for a number of reasons. In particular, a certification requirement that courses delivered by video must be delivered in real time, across time zones, and corresponding to myriad class bell schedules proved extremely difficult to fulfill. Working with local bureaucracies proved daunting, as well.

As I've noted, the U.S. Department of Education's Star Schools Program has succeeded in providing real-time video for primary and secondary schools in the United States.

It's a program to watch closely. As Knowledge TV and its affiliates do in higher education, Star Schools is helping document and shape the role of technology and telecommunications in primary and secondary schools.

WHAT'S NEXT?

What's next for Knowledge TV? Depending on whose statistics you choose, there are either 900 million[8] or 1 billion[9] television sets in the world. Even in remote regions of the world, where telephone service is limited, there is at least one television set — usually located in a town's gathering place. Knowledge TV will continue to extend its reach to those areas. Through electronic platforms, Knowledge TV can direct its product, courseware from the world's universities, to virtually anyone, anywhere. Knowledge TV's recent agreement to provide programming to China is a case in point.

Knowledge TV's approach to higher education will continue to be one of augmentation, not replacement, of existing educational institutions. Knowledge TV firmly embraces the academic environment and extends it. Universities have different structures. Those structures haven't changed much for hundreds of years. With Knowledge TV, IUC, and ICC, we're simply introducing a paradigm shift.

With respect to cable technology, what's next — in fact what's now — is the cable modem. It transmits the complex graphical images that take seemingly forever to download onto your home computer 100 to 1,000 times faster than any current modem connected to telephone lines. The exact speed is determined by the amount of traffic traveling the Internet at the time the material is being downloaded. Cable modems work over the same combination of fiber-optic and coaxial cable that allows cable television subscribers to view Knowledge TV and the rest of the vast array of commercial programming accessible via cable. Theoretically, a cable modem can pump data into homes or offices at rates of nearly 10 million bits per second. When you use a cable modem to link to the Internet, the Internet becomes like television — just point and click and you're there.

Cable modems currently are expensive: $400 to $600, depending on the features they contain. And, at about 8 pounds, they're heavy, too. But, as the technology is refined and the marketplace works its magic, cable modems will become lighter and prices will likely decline dramatically.

As has been the case so far in the emerging knowledge age, it appears that the United States will be the first country to benefit fully from cable modems. Mary Modahl, Massachusetts-based Forrester Research, Inc.'s group director, says Americans' fascination with technology makes them like "the Borg," the characters first introduced on *Star Trek: The Next Generation,* who are half machine, half human.[10] Right now, more than 11,000 cable systems directly service about 60% of U.S. homes; cable lines pass by another 30% of homes that are not cable subscribers.[11] Many cable systems in the U.S. are being upgraded so that they can provide any form of interactive video, sound, or data services.

But, despite its "Borgness," the United States and nearly all other developed nations also are at a disadvantage when it comes to information highway building. We've already got a two-lane highway, so to speak — one that allows traffic to travel, albeit slowly, along copper wires for much of its journey. In the developing world, fiber-optic cable is the building material of the information highway. It will not take long for the developing world to catch up — especially if the right partnerships between governments and the private sector are forged to create the entrepreneurial solutions that will help pave the way.

The cable industry also is looking toward a more competitive marketplace as the 21st century emerges. Government regulators worldwide increasingly are opening their telecommunications infrastructures to accommodate competition. The benchmark, in fact, already has been set in the United Kingdom.

In the 1980s the U.K. government decided it would be a good idea to allow competition in its telecommunications marketplace. As a result, enlightened government policy there for the past decade or so has allowed and encouraged broadband operators — entities like cable companies — to deliver telephony and video products and services. These systems are being completed, and as a consequence the United Kingdom will have the most luxuriant, ubiquitously available electronic platform in existence. The rest of the world will have to compete with it.[12]

The United States followed suit with its Telecommunications Act of 1996, which at this writing is working its way through the U.S. Federal Communications Commission's rule-making process.

Other countries are in the process of selling government-owned telephone companies to private-sector telephone service providers.

As competition takes hold in the world telecommunications marketplace, costs are expected to decrease and consumers will benefit. It is happening in the United Kingdom now, it will happen in the United States, and, ultimately, if the trend continues, it will happen around of the world. This can only bode well for distance education students and providers.

---

[1]Robert L. Hilliard, *Television and Adult Education* (Cambridge, Mass.: Schenkman Books, Inc., 1985), 122.

[2]Gene Koretz, "The Boom in Adult Education," *Business Week,* 10 July 1995, 24.

[3]John Elson, "The Campus of the Future," *Time,* 13 April 1992, 54.

[4]Jacques Delors, "Education for Tomorrow," *The UNESCO Courier* (April 1996), 9.

[5]Asher Deleon, " 'Learning to be' in retrospect," *The UNESCO Courier* (April 1996), 11.

[6]Robert Bisaillon, "Schools at the Crossroads," *The UNESCO Courier* (April 1996), 26.

[7]As the use of telecourses and other video-based programs has grown, so too have the number and type of groups providing programming alternatives. Some, like Pacific Mountain Network, function as a clearinghouse of information and programs for a network of member educational institutions. Others, such as Canada-based TV Ontario, produce their own high-quality programs and sell them to educational institutions around the world.

Several of the largest providers are nonprofit consortia comprising member states' education agencies and educational television authorities. Two highly successful examples of this type of programming provider are the 12-state Satellite Telecommunications Educational Programming Network (STEP), based in Washington state, and the 19-state Satellite Educational Resources Consortium (SERC), headquartered in Columbia, S. C. Both have received Star Schools Program funding from the federal government.

Commercial program providers have stepped forward to offer other programming alternatives. These alternatives are informative and useful as supplements to in-class instruction but typically do not carry secondary school or university credit. For example, cable television operators have joined together to provide schools with newscasts from CNN, as well as current events and other informative programming from such channels as C-SPAN, Discovery, Arts & Entertainment, Disney, and others. The cable industry has coordinated much of its efforts under the name Cable in the Classroom. Its offerings to date are without commercials and exclude, incredibly, most for-credit distance education. Knowledge TV has contributed its not-for-credit Global Library Project programming to this effort. Under Cable's High Speed Education Connection, the industry also has committed to provide free high-speed Internet access to elementary and secondary schools across the United States.

[8]"TV Viewing Soars Globally," *The Futurist* (September–October 1995).

[9]Parker Rossman, *The Emerging Worldwide Electronic University: Knowledge Age Global Higher Education* (Westport, Conn.: Greenwood Press, 1992), 139.

[10]Harvey Blume, "Touchstone," *Wired*, May 1996, 127.

[11]Wilson Dizard, *New Media/Old Media* (White Plains, N.Y.: Longman, 1994), 69.

[12]Recognition must be given here for the contributions of Jon Davey, Director of Cable and Satellite at the Independent Television Commission in the United Kingdom, clearly one of the world's most visionary, even handed perceptive and respected regulators. The United Kingdom regulatory scheme, as of this writing, I believe remains and outstanding world model.

With the development of the Internet, and with the increasing pervasiveness of communication between networked computers, we are in the middle of the most transforming technological event since the capture of fire.

—John Perry Barlow,
    in *Harper's Magazine*

6

THE INTERNET COMES TO SCHOOL

At the end of 1994, *Business Week* touted the World Wide Web as "the hippest, most exciting neighborhood on the Internet." Today, the Web is not just hip, it's mainstream. Somewhere in the graphics of nearly every television commercial or promotional announcement, there's a Web address. Even if they aren't "wired," most people in North America, Europe, many parts of Asia and South America, and some parts of Africa know that www.something.com or .org is an Internet Web address. A few "mouse" clicks and the so-called internaut is exploring the wonders of cyberspace. E-mail, as opposed to the world's postal services' "snail mail," is the accepted way to communicate.

In a true test of its acceptance, Hollywood immortalized the Internet on celluloid in the 1995 film, "The Net." Indeed, Louis Platt, president and CEO of Hewlett-Packard, calls the Internet the newest utility — right up there with water, power, and telephone service. Andrew Laursen, vice president of network computing at Oracle Corporation, says, "The Internet will subsume television, radio, and retail. The Internet will be everything."[1]

Maybe not everything. But, in distance education, the Internet truly is a transforming technology. In fact, Hudson Institute scholars Chester Finn and Bruno Manno contend that "even if we have only the PC and the Internet, we have enough to revolutionize education."[2] The point is, through electronic education delivery, it is possible to shift the emphasis in education from the institution to the student, where it belongs. And, it is possible to deliver education more cheaply. As I've mentioned, it is becoming more and more apparent everyday that fiscal concerns will shape education, its quality, and how it is delivered.

We now have the ability to organize information and manage it like we've never had before. And we have a critical need to lower the cost of education. We must strengthen education institutions — it's in everyone's interest — and at the same time realize that the notion of education institutions as physical places — real estate, if you will — is diminishing. Everyone in higher education will be impacted by the Internet, including college presidents, regents, and faculty members. The Internet allows smaller classes and more one-on-one interaction with students, via electronic chat rooms and e-mail. Finn and Manno envision an on-line education resource where "course lectures are available not in 50-minute chunks but in 2- to 5-minute video segments closely matched to a paragraph of the textbook and a video of an expensive-to-duplicate demonstration, with problem sets right at hand."[3]

THE FUTURE IS HERE

Manno and Finn's vision is already a functional reality. Currently there are many distance learning certificate and university degree courses offered via the Internet and World Wide Web that use combinations of video, e-mail, on-line chat groups, and text-based materials. In fact, there now is an entire book devoted to cataloguing Internet-based higher education worldwide,[4] and a quick browse through the Web reveals on-line public and private university offerings galore.

In the United States, through Pennsylvania State University's virtual classroom, students can take courses such as the popular on-campus "History of Sexuality," "Grant Writing Tips for Health Care Professionals," and "A Nurses Guide to the Internet." Long a leader in distance education, Penn State has used e-mail in its independent study courses since early 1995. Check out Penn State's on-line programs at http://www.cde.psu.edu/de/catalog/. Indiana University offers its journalism students electronic field trips to the Cable News Network center in Atlanta. They also can access journalism periodicals from all over the world.[5]

While these cyberspace course offerings are groundbreaking, they don't offer a student the ability to get a degree on-line. There are other universities that do, however. Indeed, largely as a result of the Internet's incredibly speedy absorption into the fabric of human communication options, the worldwide electronic university now is possible. Currently ConnectEd, the spin-off from New York City's New School, has offered for several years an on-line master's degree program in communications taught by faculty from Tokyo to Cape Cod. There also is an impressive project slated to get underway at the California State University at San Diego called the University of the World. Plans are that it will be all-electronic.

ON-LINE PIONEERS

An on-line pioneer, the University of Phoenix (http://www.uophx.edu/) offers both undergraduate and graduate degree courses in cyberspace. All are business and technology-related. Entrance requirements are similar to those of traditional on-site universities, but with a few additions. For example, for undergraduate admission, an on-line student must have a high school diploma or the equivalent thereof, be at least 23 years old, and have had at least two years of post-high school work experience with exposure to organizational systems and management processes. In addition, students must already have amassed 24 credit hours from some other higher education institution. For graduate work, the requirements are equally rigorous.

The University of Phoenix has its own on-line education software package. Called Alexware, the school's software system works on either DOS or Macintosh computer systems. On-line students must obtain and install Alexware, have at least a 2,400 bps modem, and word processing and spreadsheet programs. There's a computer conferencing system for on-line class discussions. Class size is limited to 13.

(No distance learning class should have more than 25 students per tutor or instructor, according to distance education expert Paul Levinson, head of ConnectEd.[6])

Terri Hedegaard, vice president of on-line programs at the University of Phoenix, says the school's on-line effort has been successful. After eight years in operation, "we think we're there," she says. "For us it began as an outreach method. We picked the [on-line] medium because it's very supportive of the adult teaching/learning process. It's interactive, which is the way adults learn."

WORLDWIDE LEARNING REVOLUTION

The on-line learning revolution is not confined to the United States. As early as 1993, the doyen of all distance learning higher education institutions, British Open University, was contemplating creating an electronic campus.

BOU envisions an electronic campus that offers students access not just to the Open University facilities but also to national and international libraries, databases, and other information resources. Currently, BOU On-Line (http://www.open.ac.uk/) is offering two computer science courses in which 350 students are enrolled. Here's the way the BOU on-line campus works: As part of the course materials, students are issued Trumpet Internet software, the Eudora electronic mail program, and World Wide Web browser Netscape Navigator. Assignments are submitted by students via e-mail to a mailbox at the university. A tutor — this is in essence one-on-one education — is automatically informed via e-mail that the completed assignment is in the mailbox ready for grading. BOU plans to offer the two courses on-line again in 1997.

In Latin America and other developing areas of the world, on-line and other electronic education options arguably are the most cost-effective way to educate enough of the population to bring those countries into the 21st century knowledge age. Inflation and interest on huge foreign debts are having profound impacts on education funding in that part of the world. Thirty-five years ago Latin American countries were able to send their best and brightest abroad — mostly to the United States — for graduate studies, but it is now "prohibitively expensive" to do so.[7] Likewise, building new brick-and-mortar campuses doesn't seem to be a viable option. In addition, universities in Latin America often can't afford increasingly expensive scholarly journals.

Some of the groundwork for distance education in that part of the world already has been laid. Costa Rica and Venezuela, for example, have distance education institutions: Universidad Estatal a Distancia in Costa Rica and Universidad Nacional Abierta in Venezuela. In addition, the Monterrey, Mexico, Institute of Technology, or ITSEM, (http://www.sistema.itesm.mx/) beams television courses complemented by Internet resources via satellite

26 locations in Mexico and to others throughout North and South America. The courses are taught in Spanish and English.

LIVENING UP K-12 EDUCATION

With apologies to all the world's hard working teachers, for kindergarten through 12th graders, on-line education is beginning to put new life into curricula.

Consider the Global Schoolhouse (http://www.gsn.org). It's an internationally recognized K-12 project funded through a public-private partnership that includes the National Science Foundation, Cornell University, the University of Illinois, AT&T, Cisco, Farallon, Sprint, SuperMac, and Zenith Electronics. Students in 12 U.S. states and six other countries share information on projects together. They use e-mail, the World Wide Web, and live video teleconferencing with their PCs. Projects they've worked on include alternative energy sources, solid-waste management, space exploration, and weather and natural disasters.[8]

The Global Schoolhouse is the brainchild of Global School Net Foundation, a 501(c)(3) nonprofit corporation, which wants to be known as a major contributor to the "philosophy, design, culture, and content of educational networking on the Internet and in the classroom," according to Global School House's home page on the World Wide Web. From its beginnings more than 10 years ago by school teachers in San Diego, Calif. — with no budget and minimal support — Global School Net has emerged as an internationally recognized piece of the global education infrastructure.

Then there's KIDLINK, founded by Odd de Presno, a Norwegian journalist and author of computer books. KIDLINK is sort of a global kids kaffeklatch, where kids from classrooms all over the world can discuss topics, through the KIDFORUM, such as "Environment 2093," "Native Literature," and "Cost of Living."[9]

In Florida, Space Coast Middle School in Port St. John is completely wired. The school opened in August 1995 with 1,650 sixth-, seventh-, and eighth-graders. It was designed as a model technology school for the Brevard County, Fla., school district. All 80 classrooms are wired for Internet access; 300 Apple Macintoshes grace the classrooms.

In Maryland, the Montgomery County public schools have instituted a Global Access plan to electronically connect classrooms, media centers, and offices so students and staff can access information and communicate locally, through an "Intranet," and globally, via the Internet. The plan, adopted in 1993, mandates that each classroom have at least one and as many as 28 computers with software tools and access to networked resources in each school's media center. Full implementation of the Montgomery County plan is expected to take six years and cost $70 million.

In California, NetDay '96 was created and sponsored by Sun Microsystems to get 12,000 Golden State public and private schools wired for access to the Internet on March 9, 1996, using volunteers from the business community. NetDay '96 wired, to some extent, about 30 percent of the state's schools — all in one day. It was so successful North Carolina and nearly 20 other states in the United States plan to have their own net days.

The U.S. cable industry has been wiring classrooms since 1989 through its Alliance for Education initiative. Some 8,400 cable systems and 32 national cable networks have wired 75% of the U.S.'s public and private K-12 classrooms. Right now these classrooms receive free 525 hours of educational television, specifically designed for the classroom, every month.

Cable companies also are creating wide-area fiber-optic networks connecting communities' education resources in rural and urban U.S. locations.

For example, in Mercer County, New Jersey, Comcast Cable Communications, Inc., and a 14-member local education consortium have created MercerNet. It will link all Mercer County school districts, Mercer Community College, and a local science center with one another and with each of the county's public libraries and state colleges.

The network will provide interactive TV for distance learning and community programs, high-speed cable access to the Internet, and high-speed data connectivity via cable, interfaced with multimedia video libraries in and out of the United States. With help from a $700,000 grant from the National Telecommunications and

Information Administration, 14 interactive video classrooms with multiple-data channels will be connected to MercerNet.

Similar projects are underway in South Dakota, Louisiana, Michigan, Kentucky, Virginia, and California.

Also in California is the fledgling and private Cyber High School (http://www.webcom.com/~cyberhi), a high school that resides entirely in cyberspace.[10] Lessons and tests are delivered by e-mail or on-line in real time. Many of the resources used in Cyber High's classes are found on the Net. At this writing, the school was applying for accreditation by the Western Association of Schools and Colleges.

ON-LINE LEARNING IN CANADA

Canada, long known as a leader in distance education because of its far-flung population, has Internet-delivered and complemented courses in secondary schools throughout its provinces. For example, for the past three years British Columbia's New Directions in Distance Learning project (http://www.etc.bc.ca) has used Internet tools to teach 20 subjects to 11th- and 12th-graders in 30 schools in the province. While New Directions doesn't use the World Wide Web yet, it is piloting some options based on the Web. The project uses a Canadian software product called First Class to interface between the Internet and its on-line service. First Class allows services like e-mail and bulletin board systems and provides a computer conferencing environment, among other things.

The New Directions in Distance Learning project also provides real-time instruction on-line, allowing students and teachers to sequentially manipulate mathematical formulas, for example, in an electronic environment. New Directions in Distance Learning teaches very few courses entirely on-line, however. Most courses include printed materials; communication between students and teachers is on-line.

THE QUESTION OF ACCESS

While the effort to get primary and secondary school classrooms in the United States wired is commendable, the question remains whether enough potential distance learners are able to use the Internet or other on-line systems, not just in North America, but worldwide.

There's good news and bad news on this subject. The statistics on Internet usage are impressive. In 1985, for example, there were only 300,000 registered e-mail users worldwide. In 1993, there were 12 million people who used e-mail and other on-line services just in the United States.[11] In 1996, the figure in the United States is closer to 80 million. Twenty years ago only 50,000 computers existed in the entire world. In early 1996, more than 50,000 computers were sold worldwide every 10 hours.[12] While the United States has the highest computer-per-person ratio in the world, at one for approximately every three people, Canada's ratio is not far behind, at one for every four Canadians, and Australia's is slightly higher. The United Kingdom boasts a ratio of one for every five of its citizens. And in Hong Kong, the computer-per-person ratio is projected to more than double — from one for about every eight people to one for about every three people — between now and 2000.[13]

That's the good news.

The bad news is that even in the United States there is a long row to hoe before Internet access is truly ubiquitous. At the end of 1995, only 35% of the United States' public schools had access to the Internet; only 3% of that nation's public school classrooms were connected.[14]

Another disturbing statistic often is tossed into conversations about technology by telecommunications analysts: Only half the world's population has ever made a telephone call.

In the United States, rural and inner city public primary and secondary schools have the least access to computers and Internet access. A recent article in *Newsweek* magazine illustrated this circumstance all too clearly. The story was about a California-based high tech chip maker, MIPS, that wanted to help rural and inner city schools gain access to the Internet. MIPS gave more than $55,000 to a school in Brooklyn, New York. The school didn't use it to buy computers. "They had a more urgent need," the article reported. The school administrators used the money to buy desks and chairs.[15]

The story points out some glaring inequities in today's U.S. schools to be sure, but make no mistake, the trend toward using the latest telecommunications technology in teaching — either on-site or at a distance and at every level — is no passing fad. Soon cost may no longer be considered a barrier, either, at least in the developed world. Not when Oracle Corporation has developed a $500 network computer — about the cost in the United States of a decent color television. Attach it to a cable or phone line and a modem, download information from the Internet, and the Internaut distance learner is in business.

WHAT'S NEXT?

Is there something out there in the ether that will revolutionize distance learning beyond the new horizons of the Internet and the World Wide Web? How about "smart card" technology? A smart card looks like your garden variety credit card, but it's capable of tracking and organizing a distance education student's learning programs "with the same degree of efficiency and pervasiveness as credit cards track individual finances."[16]

As personal communication systems (PCS) replace telephones, allowing everyone in the world to have the same phone number for their whole lives, smart cards will become the way individuals access and interact with all manner of information, experts predict. For example, let's say you are on vacation in Germany and need to check up on an assignment for which you've forgotten the due date. Attached to your PCS is a smart card with a micro electronic circuit that keeps track of, among other things, your educational progress. Slip it into a smart card "reader" or perhaps a computer terminal, and it will reveal the current status of all your course work.

And, according to Barry Barlow, an education technology expert at the University of Saskatchewan, smart card technology will be interactive. Most of the work on smart card technology is being done in Europe.

What about virtual reality? Virtual reality is "a complete environment" that is assembled and managed by a computer software program. Instead of manipulating two-dimensional images while sitting at a keyboard, the virtual reality participant dons a special interface — right now a pair of goggles — that allows him or her to become part of a three-dimensional program.[17] For example, ScienceSpace, an evolving "suite of virtual worlds" that helps students master difficult science concepts, has been created by Chris Dede and his colleagues at the Graduate School of Education at George Mason University in Virginia.[18] Dede says virtual reality is more like diving into an aquarium as opposed to looking at fish and fauna through the aquarium's window.

Three virtual worlds currently are in various stages of completion at George Mason:

- NewtonWorld, which allows students to dive into the world of one-dimensional motion;

- MaxwellWorld, which puts students inside electrostatics; and

- PaulingWorld, which allows students to experience molecular structure from the inside out.

By becoming part of the phenomenon, virtual learners gain "direct experiential intuitions about how the natural world works," Dede contends.

Then there's the Remote Exploratoriums project at the University of Colorado, Boulder. Using a programming environment called Agentsheets, Remote Exploratoriums are designed to take students navigating the World Wide Web beyond the passive role of viewing to the active role of building artifacts. Learning environments already developed include a simulation world on the Web for electric circuits, a model of melting ice, and a virtual ocean ecology.[19]

The new technology is out there. It's all possible. What makes sense for distance educators to use remains to be determined. It is hoped the technology that can provide the greatest access to education for the greatest number will be at the top of distance educators' shopping lists worldwide.

---

[1]Nikhil Hutheesing, "Web Snarl," *Forbes*, 8 April 1996, 100.

[2]Chester E. Finn and Bruno Manno, "What's Wrong With the American University?" *Wilson Quarterly*, 20 (winter 1996), 48.

[3]Ibid.

[4]Dan Corrigan, *The Internet University: College Courses by Computer* (Harwich, Mass.: Cape Software Press, 1996).

[5]Eric C. Richardson, "Internet Cum Laude," *Internet World*, October 1995, 41.

[6]Parker Rossman, *The Emerging Worldwide Electronic University: Knowledge Age Global Higher Education* (Westport, Conn.: Greenwood Press, 1992), 10.

[7]Rossman, *Worldwide Electronic University*, xiii.

[8]John R. Vacca, "CU on the Net," *Internet World*, October 1995, 81.

[9]G. Davies and B. Samways, eds., "KIDLINK, Creating the Global Village" *Teleteaching*, (North-Holland: Elsevier Science Publishers, B.V., 1993), 837.

[10]Corrigan, *Internet University*, 85.

[11]Emilio Gonzalez, *"Connecting the Nation: Classrooms, Libraries and Health Care Organizations in the knowledge age"* (U.S. Department of Commerce, 1995), 4.

[12]Ibid.

[13]Jeffrey Young, "I.Q. Wars," *Forbes ASAP*, 4 December 1995, 78.

[14]Gonzalez, *Connecting the Nation*, 10.

[15]David A. Kaplan and Adam Rogers, "The Silicon Classroom," *Newsweek*, 22 April 1996, 60.

[16]Barry Willis, ed., *Distance Education: Strategies and Tools* (Englewood Cliffs, N. J.: Educational Technology Publications, Inc., 1994), 32.

[17]Ibid., 226.

[18]See a prepublication version of Chris Dede's "Emerging Technologies and Distance Learning" written in January 1996 for *The American Journal of Distance Education.*

[19]Ibid.

The open society, the unrestricted access to knowledge, the unplanned and uninhibited association of men for its furtherance – these are what may make a vast, complex, ever growing, ever changing, ever more specialized and expert technological world, nevertheless a world of human community.

7

—J. Robert Oppenheimer,
  in *Science and the Common Understanding*

DISTANCE LEARNING: DEFINING THE MARKET

Where there is a need, there usually is a market. Distance education is no exception.

The global market for distance education delivery is burgeoning, be it via satellite and cable to television sets or via telephone line and the Internet to computers. Estimates are that distance learning in the United States alone will be an $825 million industry by 1997. That would be an increase of more than 77% since 1992–93. Worldwide, the distance education market is estimated at $8.25 billion.[1] When we look at the developing world's need for education, we see that those estimates for 1997 are just the tip of the iceberg.

China's higher education infrastructure illustrates my point. The higher education system in China counts about 2,000 universities, colleges and adult education institutions that enroll between 4.5 million and 5 million full-time and part-time students in both bachelor's degree and non-degree programs. However, there are some 80 million young people in China ages 18 to 22 years old. If 40% of them were to pursue higher education (about

68% of U.S. high school graduates enter college), that would be 32 million students vying for 5 million spaces.[2] And this projection takes into account only the student learners, not any older adults seeking higher education. Attempting a rough estimate of potential adult learners in China, whose population at last count was 1.2 billion, brings the total potential distance learners in just that one Asian country exponentially higher.

There are challenges, to be sure, in delivering electronically based higher education to different parts of the world. For example, in China TVs are commonplace in almost every urban home. Computers and connections to the Internet are not. In Japan and Korea, delivering higher education on the Internet is not a problem, although overcoming the language barrier presented by English-based education is.

In India, which has the expertise and technological savvy and where English is either the first or second language for many people, the caste system creates barriers for many potential distance learners.

The issue for all of Asia — with the exception of India, Australia, New Zealand, and a few others — is that the culture of learning is different. It is, by and large, one way, from teacher to student, and is based more on memorization than is U.S.-style higher education. It is necessary to keep this in mind when developing distance education courses that bridge Western and Asian cultures.

Australia and New Zealand, it should be noted, are long-time leaders in distance education. The market in both countries is both wired and proven.

In the rest of English-speaking East Asia — Singapore, Malaysia, parts of Indonesia, Hong Kong, and the Philippines — there is an enormous demand for higher education. With the exception of Hong Kong and Singapore, however, there is not yet sufficient information technology infrastructure to provide distance education from an electronic platform to those who desire it.

There is demand in Europe, although the potential student population is smaller. British Open University provides the potential for higher education at a distance to nontraditional students from all over the European Union.[3]

The marketplace also is substantial in South America and Africa. While the population is large and growing, the telecommunications and cable infrastructure is less ubiquitous. It will take some time for the technology to become widespread. When it does, however, the market will boom.

In Europe, the challenges facing distance education are cultural, not technical. Especially in eastern Europe, computers are part of the furnishings in the homes of most of the intelligentsia. Satellite technology is advanced all over Europe. As in the United States, TV is everywhere. But Europe in general does not have a tradition of promoting open access to education — despite the great success of British Open University.

In Africa, the challenges are political, social, and economic. In the mostly Muslim north, there is a small group that can afford to tap into technology-delivered distance learning. But, in general, the masses of people in that region don't have access. In addition, many of the countries are politically unstable.

In central Africa, the same factors are at work, but to an even greater extent. Only one country in the region can be considered even moderately stable: Kenya. And the percentage of the population that can afford more than the most basic standard of living is miniscule.

In South Africa, the situation is better. According to Marjorie Peace Lenn, head of the Washington, D.C.-based Center for Quality Assurance in International Education, at least 25% of the country is ready to receive technology-delivered distance education. It's interesting to note, however, that South Africa has only had television since the mid-1980s.

For generations, South Africa's black and colored population was provided with less than adequate education under the policies of apartheid. Now, the South African government hopes to remedy the public education deficit using distance education technology. But first things first. Many rural areas and townships have first to receive electricity.

Africa is getting some help on the technology-based distance education front from at least one international organization, however. The World Bank is working on a project to create a virtual university that would cover the entire continent.

In North America, the United States and Canada are wired, and the market for distance education is huge and proven. In Mexico, the Monterrey Institute of Technology is leading the way with satellite delivered and Internet-augmented distance education. Mexican professors also have their own listserv on the Internet, called Profmex. Even though there is the cultural barrier of an entrenched class system in Mexico, the last two elected governments in that country have voiced a commitment to universal education.

In Central America and South America, politics, culture, and technology access are the challenges. Central America, which includes the Caribbean, has a significant English-speaking population, but politics are turbulent and universal access to technology is a distant goal. In South America, with the exception of Chile, the same challenges apply, while the languages are Spanish and Portuguese. In addition, faculty unions in universities are entrenched and powerful. Although many faculty members are exploring electronic platform delivery, many others do not welcome technology-based distance education.

Despite these hurdles, however, I believe information highway technology will be available in most parts of this vast planet sooner than most people think. Among others taking this optimistic view is A. W. Bates, executive director for research and strategic planning at the Open Learning Agency in British Columbia, Canada, who in 1993 predicted that within the next 10 years the integration of computers, television, and telecommunications through both digitization and compression techniques would become commonplace.

He also predicted the costs for such integrated systems would go down. In March 1996, U.S. computer maker Gateway 2000 introduced Destination, a combination TV-computer for the home market.[4] The new machine uses a Pentium chip-based personal computer with special accessory cards for high-quality sound and video and is attached to a 31-inch computer monitor. It comes with a wireless keyboard and a remote control. At the time Destination was launched, suggested retail price was $3,800. According to several consumer industry analysts, this is only the first of what is expected to be a flood of convergent technology big-screen home computer/video systems that will effectively place classrooms, laboratories, and professors' offices into the living rooms of the world.[5]

A CAMPUS FOR EVERY CONTINENT

In 1966 the most advanced transatlantic telephone cable could carry only 138 simultaneous conversations between Europe and North America. In 1988, the first fiber-optic cable carried 40,000

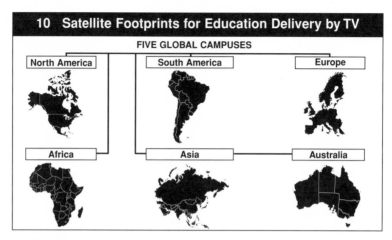

simultaneous conversations. The fiber-optic cables of the 1990s can carry nearly 1.5 million.[6]

In early 1996, with current satellite technology, it is possible to beam distance learning programs to every continent of the world. In fact, the mission of Jones Education Company's Knowledge TV is to create five electronic campuses using five existing telecommunications satellites. The campuses' reach will replicate the satellites' footprints on Earth[7] and it will all be under-girded with the Internet.

Envisioned are the North American campus, reaching from the Panama Canal to the Arctic Circle; the South American campus, reaching south to Cape Horn; the European campus, reaching from northern Europe past the boot of Italy and into parts of North Africa; the African campus, reaching south to cover the rest of the continent; and the Asian campus, reaching from the north of the Asian continent to Australia and the South Pacific.

The infrastructure to pick up satellite signals is multiplying. In the subcontinent of India alone, the number of cable TV-equipped homes receiving satellite channels almost doubled between 1993 and 1994, from 7.5 million to 14 million. By 2000, India expects to have 80 million cable TV-equipped homes able to receive up to 250 digitally compressed services.[8]

WORLDWIDE ELECTRONIC CORPORATE EDUCATION AND TRAINING

Higher education delivered electronically worldwide is not just constrained to the kind that culminates in a university degree. It also can work for executive education and training. In that realm, the education delivery pendulum is swinging toward technology at an ever increasing rate. Corporations, now lean and mean, can't afford the luxury of sending managers to one- or two-week training programs off site. Indeed, *Business Week* magazine quoted one U.S. CEO as saying, "If we can do without someone for a week, we can probably do without them for good."[9] As a result, while less than 20% of training currently is delivered by technology, *Corporate University Xchange*, an industry newsletter, forecasts that by 2000 more than 50% will be delivered by some mix of videotapes, audio tapes, CD-ROMS, interactive video conferencing, satellite-delivered training, and training on the Internet.[10] U.S. corporations alone spend about $30 billion on executive education and training — roughly 1.4% of their payrolls. This percentage jumps to 2.5% if the U.S. corporation is among the Fortune 500.[11]

In Japan and Germany, the portion of an employee's time dedicated to education and training runs between 8% and 10%.

WHO'S DELIVERING DISTANCE CORPORATE EDUCATION?

Universities, nonprofits, and public-private partnerships are beginning to beam corporate education and training almost everywhere. The delivery modes vary from real-time, video-based instruction to computer-based virtual training programs.[12]

Here are a few examples:

Executive Education Network. One of the more recently formed public-private executive education and training collaborations to use technology to deliver its product is the Executive Network (EXEN). Carrollton, Texas-based Westcott Communications, Inc. runs the network. Twelve universities and institutes provide the programming. They include Babson College, the Universities of Southern California, North Carolina, Massachusetts, Notre Dame, and Texas and the Aspen Institute, to name a few.

The courses are delivered in real time via satellite to a company's work site or corporate classroom facility. The technology is interactive. Manager-students watch the course instructor on a video screen and can speak to him or her via a microphone in a keypad.

While instructors can't see the puzzled looks on students' faces, they know when they aren't getting a point across because students can push the "flag" button on their keypads. The number of flag buttons pushed at any one time is calculated and revealed to the off-site instructor on a computer screen. EXEN provides the hardware. At the end of 1995, EXEN had more than 100 corporate classrooms set up at companies in the United States.

EXEN also has classrooms in Canada and expects to expand to Europe and the Pacific Rim in 1997. At this writing, talks were underway with the London School of Business and the Monterrey Institute of Technology to provide additional course content for EXEN's training programs.

Jones Education Company. Jones Education Company (JEC), a subsidiary of Jones International, also delivers corporate education and training.

The courses are delivered through a combination of satellite, cable, video, and Internet-based technologies. Manager-students communicate via e-mail, electronic chat rooms, and voice mail. The courses aren't confined to delivery in real time and customized equipment such as interactive keyboards isn't necessary. As a result, the programming can be delivered to more than one location at a time.

Manager-students take management training courses, including master's and MBA-level curriculum at home or at work, on their own schedules. International University College (IUC) and International Community College (ICC), both non-profit institutions that are part of the Jones organization, work with industry partners to develop degree and certificate programs.

As I've mentioned, Jones Education Company and its local partner, China Education Television, are delivering part of the course content for a computer-training series to be broadcast to 200 million viewers in China.

In Barbados, Canada, and Antigua, and at Mercedes Benz and Siemens A.G. in Germany students also are taking MBA-level courses from the University of Colorado at Colorado Springs through Knowledge TV.

National Technological University. Another work site-delivered electronic corporate education program is National Technological University. Since 1984, Fort Collins, Colo.-based NTU has offered courses and graduate degree programs to engineers via satellite. NTU is a consortium of university departments of engineering. It is run as a private, nonprofit corporation and is governed by a board of trustees, most of whom represent industry.

Faculty are located on their respective university campuses, and students take courses at their work sites. Classes are televised on multiple channels 24 hours a day, seven days a week. Most courses are recorded at the students' work sites for use at their convenience.

NTU students use e-mail, fax, telephone, and conventional mail to interact with instructors. They are able to take advantage of the combined expertise of engineering faculty at such U.S. universities as Arizona State, Alabama, California, Colorado, Maryland, Michigan, Minnesota, and Columbia, Cornell, Purdue, and Rensselaer Polytechnic Institute, to name a few of the 48 participating universities. NTU is financed through student tuition.

In early 1996, NTU began offering its degree programs internationally via satellite. Twenty universities in Thailand, the International Medical College and Motorola in Malaysia, a university in Indonesia, several locations in Australia, and Motorola in Korea now receive NTU's courses. NTU's satellite delivery footprint covers the entire Pacific Rim.

The biggest challenge so far for NTU's international expansion has been language. In Malaysia and Australia, where English is spoken, there is no problem. But in Thailand, NTU courses will probably have to be "language-mediated" for the foreseeable future.

Europace. NTU was the model for a similar consortium of universities in Europe called Europace. It serves technical professionals in European industry via satellite. Europace's satellite footprint covers 18 countries in which there are 329,000 education institutions and a population of potential learners of about 44 million. However, Europace offers non-credit instruction, not degrees.

Ford Motor Company. Many corporations create their own electronically based "corporate universities" to deliver education and training worldwide. Ford Motor Company, for example, has its own satellite-delivered closed-circuit television network, FordStar, the largest privately owned satellite network in the world, according to Ford. It was designed and developed specifically to deliver training and information programming to Ford dealerships in North America and, ultimately, around the world.

Right now, the network has more than 2,000 receiving sites in North America. Ford also uses similar satellite TV technology to deliver two training programs to 10 manufacturing sites in North America.

Ford also is piloting an on-line management training course over its in-company Intranet. The course, on effective meeting planning and management, will be targeted to between 500 and 600 Ford employees.

For Ford, the driver behind piloting the Intranet-based training program and other electronic platform-based distance education and training is the Ford 2000 initiative. Begun in 1995, Ford 2000's objective is to integrate company programs globally. The company no longer looks at itself as made up of separate units, but as a whole organization with 300,000 employees who just happen to be located in different facilities around the world.

As a result, for Ford, distance education via electronic platforms is not a passing fad, says a supervisor in Ford's Education and Training design and development division.

"Our philosophy for the use of distance learning is that it is one platform of delivery in a family of options. We are looking at an integrated delivery strategy for learning, not an individual technology such as the Internet, video, or CD-ROM. We want to incorporate all of them into the process," the supervisor said.

U.S. UNIVERSITIES TAP THE MARKET

Back in the world of degree-granting institutions, New York University is going it alone as a provider of electronically based higher education and training. The university has created the Virtual College. It claims to be the first higher education interactive teleprogram to deliver interactive video to computers in students' homes. All course materials — video, simulations, laboratories, and readings — are digital and are accessible through a single common user interface.[13]

The Virtual College uses IBM's Lotus Notes groupware and a Lotus product called Video Notes. Students can log on anytime and communicate with classmates and instructors through an e-mail system. They also take exams and check grades on-line.

The college is not for everyone. It offers only courses that lend themselves to the use of technology. Mainly adult learners — mostly managers in mid-career — can earn an advanced professional certificate in Information Technology that is designed to prepare them for work with on-line information systems. NYU's Virtual College students have included employees from British Airways, Chemical Bank, ITT, NBC, NYNEX, and the United Nations.

Using different info-technology, the University of Michigan is offering a customized MBA degree via video conferencing to managers at Daewoo Corporation in Korea and Cathay Pacific Airways Ltd. in Hong Kong. Michigan's business school also is working with a consortium of companies to deliver live video courses in the United States, Europe, and Asia.

THE GLOBAL COURSE PROTOTYPE

Creating the content for electronically delivered international courses is no easy task. Cultural barriers in different areas of the world attest to the challenge.

Most courses are simply taught in the language and within the cultural framework of the country from which the course emanates. Others are modified for local audiences. At Mind Extension University, for example, a key component of our international programming includes global language and culture courses.

There are courses, however, that are designed from the outset for an international audience. One particular course comes to mind. In 1991, the Annenberg School of Communications and the

Corporation for Public Broadcasting joined to fund and subsequently distribute an electronically delivered course known in the United States as "Inside the Global Economy."[14] A group of educators and public television broadcasters from several countries met and collaborated on the video-based course. Besides the Annenberg/CPB group, the TELEAC Foundation of The Netherlands, the Swedish Educational Broadcasting organization, JL Productions of Chile, and the Australian Broadcasting Corporation were partners in the effort.

A 13-lesson video course was the outcome. Each lesson is based on an examination of two case studies. In addition to the 13 one-hour videos, the course requires a textbook in international economics, a course reader — created as a study guide for the course — and a software-based tutor that includes a glossary of terms, graphical analysis of data, interactive testing, forecasting simulations, and a databank of test questions keyed to the textbook chapters.

The course took three years to develop, was filmed in 20 countries, and was edited to fit the needs of each region in which it was shown. Needless to say, creating content for a worldwide audience is not an easy task. But experiments such as "Inside the Global Economy" can teach us much.

The Internet takes this kind of curriculum one step further. Because of the World Wide Web's immediacy, using the Internet to deliver courses such as "Inside the Global Economy" would

111

enable content to be constantly updated, reflecting ever-changing world economic conditions.

THE ROAD AHEAD

The road ahead for electronically based international corporate education and training is still a bit bumpy, but it is definitely paved with a mix of satellite technology, silicon, and fiber. It is a road that corporations will travel. As I've noted, they have no choice. In a shrinking world, where global competition is truly inescapable, where market economies rule, businesses worldwide must keep each one of their workers current — whether on the line or in the executive suite — with cutting-edge management and technical training.

They can do it themselves, they can contract with universities, they can contract with consortiums, or they can get involved in customized education development partnerships. But, they must train. They must educate. They must do it whether their employees are in Chicago or Calcutta.

The key to success is finding the most cost-effective, flexible way to do it.

---

[1]The U.S. market is estimated to be 5% of the world total, but is also the most technology-enabled. In the absence of research data which compiles all distance education markets on the same basis, $8.25 billion was derived by increasing the U.S. market estimate by a factor of 10.

[2]Quality Education Data (census survey), 1994; Peter Li Education Group, 1993; Anne Wujcik & Associates, 1993.

[3]G. Davies and B. Samways, eds., *Teleteaching* (North-Holland: Elsevier Science Publishers B.V., 1993), 1.

[4]Evan Ramstad, Associated Press, "Product Merges PC, TV," (Boulder, Colo.) *Daily Camera*, 24 March 1996, 1B.

[5]Ibid.

[6]Nathan Rosenberg, "Why Technology Forecasts Often Fail," *The Futurist*, July–August 1995, 17.

[7]Author unknown, "Magic Carpet Ride," *Cable and Satellite Europe*, 15 June 1995.

[8]Ibid.

[9]John A. Byrne, "Virtual B-Schools," *Business Week*, 23 October 1995, 65.

[10]Author unknown, "Corporate Universities in the Year 2000," *Corporate University Xchange*, January–February 1996, 3.

[11]Jeanne C. Meister, C*orporate Quality Universities: Lessons in Building a World-Class Work Force* (Burr Ridge, Ill., and New York: Irwin Professional Publishing, 1994), 12.

[12]Ibid.

[13]Author unknown, "NYU's Virtual College Delivers Distance Learning On Demand," *Corporate University Xchange*, March–April 1996, 6.

[14]Peter J. Dirr, "Media Review," *American Journal of Distance Education*, 9, No. 3, 1995, 85.

Some people are willing to push the envelope of education delivery. And, when they do, accreditation agencies will be there to validate all or part of it.

—Jack Allen
Southern Association of Schools
and Colleges, Decatur, Ga.

8

THE ACCREDITATION DEBATE

In an electronic environment where education, entertainment, and news blend into a phenomenon called edutainment, distance education and new concepts such as cyberschools run the risk of being characterized as something less than serious higher education.

Definitions of what is and isn't technology-based distance education can become murky to the uninitiated. Is electronically delivered distance education what you learn while watching The Discovery Channel, The History Channel, The Learning Channel, or most of what's offered on public television in the United States? Of course you learn, and often the programs are compelling and of high quality. In fact, some excellent edutainment television programming — the PBS series on the U.S. Civil War, for example — is used as part of U.S. high school and college curriculums.

But there is a critical distinction between providing electronically-delivered edutainment and providing electronically-delivered distance education. The distinction is that one is credentialed and

114

one is not. One requires examination and provides certification to students and the other doesn't.

Degree- and certificate-granting distance education programs are serious education endeavors — equally as serious as those located on college campuses. Education accreditation agencies, particularly in the United States, are beginning to officially recognize their importance and legitimacy and also their need for quality control.

PRINCIPLES OF GOOD PRACTICE

In the United States, two higher education organizations have developed what are called principles of good practice in electronically delivered distance education. They are the Western Interstate Commission for Higher Education (WICHE), Boulder, Colo., and the American Council on Education, Washington, D.C.

The 17 WICHE principles were three years in the making and are called the Principles of Good Practice for Electronically Offered Academic Degree and Certificate Programs. They are essential reading for students considering enrolling in distance education programs and for institutions interested in offering such programs. They stress the development of rigorous education outcomes, completeness of programs, adequate and appropriate interaction between students and teaching faculty, appropriate support systems and training for both students and faculty, course and student evaluations, and the importance of students' access to learning resources. WICHE's Principles of Good Practice are offered in the appendix.

The American Council on Education's principles for distance learning go into greater detail, but as available in draft form in mid-1996, generally consist of five overarching concepts:

- That distance learning activities are designed to fit the specific context for learning;
- That distance learning opportunities are effectively supported for learners through fully accessible modes of delivery and resources;
- That distance learning initiatives must be backed by an organizational commitment to quality and effectiveness in all aspects of the teaching and learning environments;
- That distance education programs organize learning around demonstrable learning outcomes, assist the learner to achieve these outcomes, and assess learner progress by reference to these outcomes;
- And, that the provider has a plan and infrastructure for using technology that supports its teaching or educational goals and activities.[1]

The American Council on Education's principles also appear in full in the appendix.

The council suggests, and I concur, that its principles of good practice should be applied beyond higher education institutions. "All those involved in the learning enterprise — including individual learners, institutions, corporations, labor unions, associations, and government agencies — will benefit from principles that provide guidance in producing high-quality education with outcomes that can be clearly assessed. Strengthening one sector will improve the effectiveness of the others and, in turn, address the learning needs of individuals and society as a whole," the council's task force said in its comments accompanying the draft of the principles released in May 1996.[2]

Numerous U.S. higher education accreditation agencies have adopted WICHE's principles. They include the Northwest Association of Schools and Colleges in Seattle, Wash.; the North Central Association of Colleges and Schools in Chicago, Ill.; and the Middle States Association of Colleges and Schools in Philadelphia, Pa. Expectations are that the American Council on Education's guidelines, still in draft form, also will be embraced. Both will guide accreditors in the increasingly frequent task of determining the quality of electronically delivered education. As Dr. Margaret Kraus of the Northwest Association of Schools and Colleges says, "The guidelines will give us stars to look out for."

ACCREDITATION: WHO CONFERS IT?

Accreditation historically has been the way for students to determine whether the institution they attend maintains certain quality standards. In most countries, the central government accredits higher education institutions. In France, for example, the federal government is the accrediting agency. In the United Kingdom, the federal government essentially supervises accreditation. In Canada, the provinces are responsible.

In the United States, the accreditation system works different-ly. Its different structure may make it a potential vehicle for certifying quality in electronically delivered international distance education. A look at the history of U.S. higher education accredi-tation provides some evidence for this notion.

Education in the United States has never been the responsibil-ity of the central government. It isn't even mentioned in the con-stitution of the country. What the 10th Amendment to the U.S. con-stitution does say, however, is that powers not explicitly given to the federal government or denied to the state governments are the province of the states. Because education nowhere is mentioned, by default it became the states' responsibility.

In the 18th and early 19th centuries, the states did almost nothing about educating their populations. Even though the first public school in the North American British colonies was created by local edict in Massachusetts in 1639, education primar-ily was the province of private institutions. It was delivered through an intricate web of private preparatory schools that prepared students for private universities. Because of its exclusive nature, education was reserved for the upper classes.

The situation changed as the country expanded to the west and its citizens became more mobile. At the end of the 18th century, in the Northwest Ordinance, passed by Congress in 1787, the federal government encouraged the founding of universities on its frontier — in wild and untamed places like Michigan. And in the first half of the 19th century, public first- and secondary-level schools proliferated as a result of decisions by states to fund them through state taxes.

Because the frontier universities had no private preparatory school system from which to garner students, they were faced with what can only be described as a recruiting problem. The dilemma was this: How were they going to convince public school students to continue their education at a university?

The solution was not long in coming from the University of Michigan through a program called the "high school visitor plan." University faculty would visit public high schools in their state and examine both students and faculty to determine whether the school's students were "university material." The Michigan Plan caught on, and soon universities throughout the Midwest were visiting high schools.

The practice became so prevalent that by the early 1900s high schools were complaining they were being overrun by state university faculty. In mock desperation, the high schools suggested the process be turned around and that colleges and universities be the institutions examined.

In fact, that is what happened.

During the first half of the 20th century a series of non-governmental, mostly volunteer, peer-review regional higher education accreditation agencies came into prominence. Today there are six for higher education: the Middle States Association of Colleges and Schools, the New England Association of Schools and Colleges, the North Central Association of Colleges and Schools, the Northwest Association of Schools and Colleges, the Southern Association of Colleges and Schools, and the Western Association of Schools and Colleges.

WORLDWIDE QUALITY STANDARDS

Because U.S. higher education accrediting bodies are non-governmental, some of their agency officials believe the U.S. could become the center for accrediting higher education programs worldwide.

"We may lead the way because we are not government affiliated. That offers an edge to the United States. We can maneuver across international boundaries without competition. We also are able to transcend politics — if that's possible," contends Dr. Jack Allen, of the Southern Association of Colleges and Schools.

The Southern Association already accredits universities in Latin America. Among those with its stamp of approval are the Monterrey Institute of Technology — with multiple campuses in Mexico and satellite courses that can be beamed almost anywhere in North America — and the University of the Americas, with campuses in Puebla and Mexico City, Mexico. The University of the Andes in Bogota, Colombia, also is an applicant for Southern Association accreditation.

GATE. There is another international accreditation vehicle in its formative stages, as well, and I am privileged to be a founder. It is called the Global Alliance for Transnational Education (GATE).

GATE was created in 1995 to develop quality assurance principles that can be used to evaluate electronically delivered education courses worldwide (http://www.edugate.org/index.shtml). The alliance's first conference was held in Denver, Colo., in that year and was attended by educators from Canada, Chile, Hungary, Ireland, New Zealand, the People's Republic of China, South Africa, the United Kingdom, and the United States. The second GATE conference convened in London in September 1996.

As businesses increasingly draw their work forces from all over the globe, and as education and training are disseminated from its vast reaches, international measures of quality — such as the ISO 9000 quality standard in international manufacturing — are a necessity. Corporations and educators are just beginning to set the agenda.

Beyond setting principles for evaluating and certifying transnational education programs, the alliance is tackling ongoing projects that include amassing a database of higher education institutions throughout the world and developing an international quality assurance directory to help corporations and agencies evaluate the education credentials of potential employees.

WHAT THE ACCREDITORS THINK

Most accreditors, in the U.S. at least, believe the fundamental principles of quality they use to judge traditional education institutions apply to electronic distance education institutions as well. For example, integrity of an institution's conduct in all its activities, honesty and accuracy, adequate financial resources to run programs, and the like are applicable to both traditional and distance education institutions.

But accreditors admit certain characteristics of distance education make it unique and will be challenges for distance education institutions and accreditors alike.

One challenge is to develop methods for determining whether students and faculty are sufficiently computer literate to either instruct or successfully complete an electronically delivered course. How does the institution know, for example, if a student enrolling in an on-line degree course in business management is sufficiently knowledgeable in the technology used to deliver the course to take the exams?

One could argue here that the same question might be asked at a traditional higher education institution about the ability of a traditional student to understand how to use the on-campus library. It's normally not an admissions requirement, but most students get the hang of it rapidly.

Other issues include student access to library resources and making arrangements for students to complete curriculums that are dropped from electronic institutions. Many accreditation agencies require traditional universities and colleges to provide an independent study option or the option of completing the curriculum at another university. It would not be difficult for a cyberschool to do the same.

And what about institutional visits by accreditors? "How do you visit an individual computer?" the Southern Association's Jack Allen quips.

Clearly, these are not insurmountable issues. The key is for distance learning institutions, be they in the public or the private sector, to be aware of the requirements and provide for their fulfillment.

The North Central Association of Colleges and Schools perhaps has had the most experience dealing with the unique qualities of distance learning programs. Since the 1970s, it has accredited electronically delivered degree programs from National Technological University and distance learning programs delivered in part via electronic means from the University of Phoenix and The Union Institute (http://www.tui.edu). Union has one of the few Ph.D.-granting distance learning programs in the world.

Accreditation agency officials in the United States believe, as I do, that the trend toward the technological delivery of higher education will continue. As Allen says, "I don't think there is any doubt about it, especially as technology gets cheap enough for everyone to have it in their home. What happens is some people push the envelope of education delivery. And when they do, accreditation associations will be there to validate part or all of it."

Pushing that envelope is the business of entrepreneurs. Those of us who are higher education entrepreneurs relish the prospect.

---

[1]Eugene Sullivan and T. Rocco, *Guiding Principles for Distance Learning in a Learning Society*, draft copy (May 1996), 4.

[2]Ibid, 2.

It is the only solution for me at this point.

—Igor Ciric, distance education student,
  formerly of Belgrade, Yugoslavia

CYBERSCHOOLS AND YOU

A HOW-TO GUIDE FOR DISTANCE LEARNERS

If you've decided that distance education is an option you would like to explore in furthering your education or training, there are several important facts to keep in mind as you look for courses of study that meet your needs.

DISTANCE EDUCATION, NOT INSTANT EDUCATION

First, distance education is not instant education. For the vast majority of for-credit courses delivered via technology, it is necessary to submit an application for admission to the program and arrange for academic records to be transferred from other education institutions you have attended. After that, you must, of course, be admitted to the distance education course or program you have applied for. Even though many cyberschools will expedite this process, to gain admission to a distance education institution, you follow much the same process as you would to gain admission to a traditional institution. If you are applying to take courses via distance education at a traditional university — for example, Pennsylvania State University in University Park, Pa., has a large distance education department — you must meet its admission standards.

A RIGOROUS WAY TO LEARN

Second, distance education is rigorous. Don't expect course work to be easier simply because it is delivered via technology. Indeed, students must not only have the ability to absorb and understand the courses' content, but also be disciplined self-starters. To an even greater extent than on a traditional college campus, no one is standing over your shoulder admonishing you to get your work done. It's up to you. And it should be. After all, you're the one getting the education.

DISTANCE EDUCATION, NOT PASSIVE EDUCATION

Third, when you are a cyberstudent, it's virtually impossible for you to be a passive learner. The approach to learning is active, not passive. In traditional classrooms, students can get by for weeks at a time sitting quietly in a chair taking notes — or not taking notes — and never actively participate with the instructor and other students. We all know this because we have all done it at some point.

In a cyberschool, students nearly always must react or provide some appropriate input to continue to the next phase of an assignment. In addition, courses are more often designed to be collaborative efforts among students than are traditional lecture hall courses. In some computerized courses, a significant part of a student's grade depends upon participation in on-line discussion groups.

A Better Way To Learn?

Fourth, learning via technology may be a better way for some students to learn.

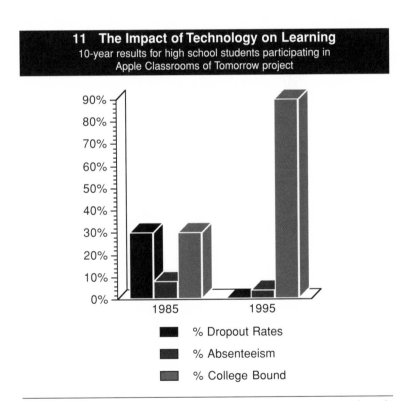

11 The Impact of Technology on Learning
10-year results for high school students participating in
Apple Classrooms of Tomorrow project

- % Dropout Rates
- % Absenteeism
- % College Bound

Source: "Teaching, Learning and Technology," a report on 10 years of ACOT Research, Apple Computer, Inc., Oct 2, 1995.

In its Apple Classrooms of Tomorrow project, Apple Computer, Inc. is investigating how teaching and learning change when people have constant access to state-of-the-art technology. The project began in 1985 and is ongoing. After the first 10 years, the project's conclusions were that students become re-energized and more excited about learning when using information technology. Grades improve, standardized test scores go up, and drop-out and absenteeism rates decrease, according to Apple's report on "Teaching, Learning and Technology." As shown in Figure 11, the study reports that over the first 10 years of the project drop-out rates for participating high school students fell from 30% to zero.

Even before the Apple project's 10-year findings, it was reported time and again in research on how we learn at all education levels that electronic instruction — either via teleconference or computer conference — can be as effective as traditional classroom-based lectures and face-to-face discussions. On-line students have test scores equal to those in conventional classrooms if the quality of the teaching is the same, they report better access to instructors, and they improved their ability to collaborate and communicate.

10 QUESTIONS TO ASK

Knowledge is power. It's a good idea to ask any distance education institution you are considering lots of questions. Here's a list of 10 to get you started.

1. **How technologically savvy do I need to be to take electronically delivered distance education courses?** It almost goes without saying that for distance learning courses delivered via technology, some degree of computer literacy is necessary. Knowledge of the Internet, especially the World Wide Web and e-mail, is a plus.

    That being said, there still are many distance education courses delivered via cable and satellite television. For those courses, knowing how to record classes from your television to a videocassette loaded in a VCR often is necessary. It also is possible in many TV courses to purchase pre-recorded videotapes of the classes. Today, however, many televised courses have an Internet component — even if that component only is using e-mail to communicate with your instructor or other classmates.

2. **What kind of information technology do I need to take these classes?** Usually a cyberschool will give you a list of the technologies that must be accessible to you when you apply for admission. Just in case a list isn't offered, you need to know whether you need access to:

    *   A computer — what kind and how powerful?
    *   A modem — what speed (how many baud's per second: 2,400? 14,400? 28,800?);
    *   Any special software;
    *   An Internet connection;

- A television equipped with cable or satellite program delivery capabilities;
- A video cassette recorder/player.

Generally, you will need to have access to some of these things. Special software, or courseware, is necessary for some distance education programs.

3. **What kind of student support structure does the institution have?** Is there a way to contact someone about course advising, or missed assignments, or student emergencies, or any other of the many questions that come up while taking courses at a distance? Is there a number to call? Is it an 800 number? Is there an e-mail address? What kind of library support services are available? Find out.

4. **Is the institution accredited?** This question is important for several reasons. First, and perhaps foremost if you are hoping to receive U.S. federal financial aid to attend classes at a cyberschool or at some less high-tech distance education institution, it's important to know that the federal government does not loan money to students attending non-accredited institutions. Similar restrictions apply in other countries. In addition, while accreditation is not absolutely necessary for a school to stay in business and award certificates and degrees, for a student a degree or certificate from an accredited institution is far and away more prestigious. Primarily because they all are so new, many cyberschools are going through the accreditation process now, and their applications are being carefully scrutinized.

According to accreditors in the United States, technologically delivered education is legitimate and if not already recognized by a particular accrediting agency, it soon will be. For more information about accreditation, see Chapter 8.

5. **Is a degree I get from a cyberschool based in a country in which I'm not a citizen going to be recognized?** In the near future, the answer to this question will more than likely be yes. Right now, among other international efforts, there is some cross-border accreditation occurring between the United States and Mexico and the United States and Colombia. In addition, there is an international education group called the Global Alliance for Transnational Education (GATE) that is working on international distance education standards and an international education database. The database will contain information about universities and their programs around the world. For more information on GATE and cross-border accreditation, see Chapter 8.

Remember, for years students have gone to traditional universities in one country — for a bachelor's degree, for example — and with few if any problems continued their graduate education in universities in another country.

6. **Where do I buy the textbooks required for the course?** Textbooks still are part and parcel of any education. Make sure you know how and where to obtain yours.

7. **Are the instructors at the cyberschool trained to teach on-line?** A very important question to ask because teaching in cyberspace requires a different, more interactive approach than teaching to students in a classroom.

8. **Is it possible to complete an entire degree program via technology through this institution?** Again, to effectively plan your education strategy, knowledge of how much you can complete on-line or via video is important.

9. **How long does it take to get a degree or certificate through this institution?** The answer may be the same amount of time it takes to complete a course of study at a traditional university, or it may be less. Often the timing is flexible, because one of the the essences of good distance education is that it allows the student to be in charge of the process. There also may be minimum and maximum allowable times. Check out your options.

10. **What if I start a degree program and find out when I'm in the middle of it that the program has been discontinued?** The vast majority of degree granting institutions — whether they be cyberschools or traditional universities — make provisions for alternative ways to complete degree programs that have been dropped. Such provisions are required for an institution to be accredited. Find out what alternatives the institution in which you plan to enroll can offer you if it discontinues your degree program.

CYBERSTUDENT OPINIONS

Beyond asking questions, another excellent way to judge the quality of a cyberschool or other type of technology-delivered distance education institution is to listen to those who have gone through a program before you.

As I've mentioned throughout this book, students enrolled in distance education courses represent diverse backgrounds, a broad range of ages, and widely varied goals.

Many are striving to enhance their career opportunities or to attain other personal and professional objectives. Some audit courses simply out of curiosity or a commitment to lifelong learning. All cite distance teaching's focus on the student as a primary factor in their decisions to take advantage of this nontraditional way to learn.

Following are several profiles of distance education students that might prove enlightening.

While the profiles by no means represent the varied and plentiful distance learning programs available around the world, I hope they will help illustrate my point that the marriage between distance learning and information technology is living up to its promise as a way to make all the world a school — one that many millions more can afford.

133

Igor Ciric, Toronto, Ontario, Canada, and Belgrade, Yugoslavia
Master's in Business Communication — in progress
International University College

Igor Ciric is a mechanical engineer, originally from Belgrade, Yugoslavia.

At this writing, Ciric is studying on-line at International University College for his master's degree in business communication. He already has finished courses in the fundamentals of business writing and basic public speaking.

His professional objective is to enhance not only his knowledge, but to add to his fields of expertise. Like many distance education students he also wants his education credentials to lead to a successful business career.

He says his experiences with distance learning thus far are highly positive. "I have all the aids for learning at home and immediate assistance from professors by e-mail." The only difficulty Ciric sees with learning at a distance is the time it requires.

"I usually come (home) from work around 5:30 p.m., so I don't have much time left for all other activities. Studies need time and concentration, so sometimes days are pretty tough and it gets very hard to meet the deadlines for assignments."

But, would he take courses via distance education again?

"Yes, I would. It is the only solution for me at this point."

Rejane Lamounier Franca
Brookline, Mass., and Belo Horizonte, Brazil
Certificate in Business Technology — in progress
International University College

Rejane Lamounier Franca is a marketing analyst for Audiolab Sistemas Eletronicos of Brazil. She is in the United States to scout opportunities for her company in the American marketplace, especially the software market. She is interested both personally and professionally in distance learning.

"Distance learning is a reality here (in the United States), and I have a great interest in seeing how it works. It's part of my business plan," Franca says.

She is working toward a certificate in Business Technology via distance education at IUC. She would be interested in getting a master's degree through IUC, but she's not sure whether she can get an Internet connection in her home country to continue her studies. If she can, she would take distance education courses again, she says.

Franca says her experience with distance learning has been positive. "So far, so good. This is my first course and I'm very impressed."

Mandy Caird
Denver, Colo.
Certificate of Course Completion,
Virtual School of Natural Sciences
Globewide Network Academy

While working in medical research at a major U.S. university health sciences center, Mandy Caird discovered cyberschools. The neurology laboratory where she was a researcher received tremendous amounts of DNA-related data, and she needed more education to analyze the statistical significance of the data. "I wasn't necessarily looking for courses on-line," she says. But that's where she found one to suit her needs — in the Virtual School of Natural Sciences, run jointly by the Massachusetts Institute of Technology and Bielefeld University in Germany through the Globewide Network Academy (http://uu-gna.mit.edu:8001/uu-gna/index.html).

The course was taught completely via the Internet, in a virtual classroom with instructions given by e-mail. The 30 to 40 people enrolled were split into groups of six and each group had its own electronic "chat room."

"My teacher was in Mexico City," Caird says. Students were from Finland, Australia, and the United States. The course was taught in real time and used shareware.

Caird says she doesn't think the course was too high-tech for the computer literate student. She does say, however, that the technological applications required to take it make it more appropriate for those with powerful computers and Internet access at home or at a traditional university.

Pablo Lucas
Hollywood, Fla.
Bachelor's, Business Administration
Regis University-Knowledge TV
Master's, Management Information Systems — in progress

Pablo Lucas began his higher education in the traditional way. A Florida resident, he first received an associate's degree from a community college in that state and then began working on a computer engineering degree at Florida International University (FIU).

He switched his major and his university when he discovered he could finish his bachelor's and get a master's degree through a distance education program in the time it would take him to graduate with only a bachelor's degree from FIU.

Lucas became Denver, Colo.-based Regis University's first graduate in one of the distance education degree programs it offers through ME/U. He began a master's degree program in Management Information Systems in January 1996.

Lucas says distance learning provided him a better education than the traditional model, because, he believes, he learned more and retained more information. He says he appreciated the difficult, hands-on projects he was required to complete.

For Lucas, the best aspects of distance education are its flexibility and its cost. "My biggest concerns [about] returning to school were the time and money it requires. [Distance education] made these obstacles minimal issues."

Lorraine Priest
Warren, Mich.
Master's in Business Administration — in progress
University of Phoenix On-line

Lorraine Priest is an information systems analyst at General Motors (GM). She has received all her academic degrees on-line. At this writing, she is finishing up the final course for her MBA at the University of Phoenix's on-line campus.

She tried to go to college "on the ground," but it didn't work. "It was too regimented. I couldn't raise a family and work and go to school," she says.

She rates her on-line collegiate experience as excellent.

For potential distance learning students who might not be cyber-wise, Priest provides some advice and comfort. "All you need to know is how to turn on your [computer]. Nowadays most of the software is very intelligent and there is always a person around to help you," she says.

Help from work and family is a plus. GM has a tuition assistance program that helped Priest with school expenses. And "my husband has done every bit of my laundry since I started school," she says.

When Priest has completed her MBA, she plans to embark on an on-line Ph.D. program through the Fielding Institute (http://www.fielding.edu) in Santa Barbara, Calif.

The whole of science is nothing more than a refinement of everyday thinking.

—Albert Einstein,
in *Physics and Reality*

10

FREE MARKET FUSION: ONE PATH

The electronic delivery of education is an ideal prospect for a process of public/private partnership I call Free Market Fusion, a management process I have studied for several years. It was chosen as the final topic for this book because it offers students, teachers, and public and private education planners a way of thinking about how they might find the resources to pursue electronic education.

This chapter also serves as a preview of my forthcoming book, *Free Market Fusion*, which treats the subject in more depth and explores several case studies. A companion preview, with interactive exercises, is available on the World Wide Web at http://www.freemarketfusion.com.

DEFINING FREE MARKET FUSION

What is Free Market Fusion? It is an entrepreneurial approach to identifying (or creating) opportunities for innovative solutions.

In physics, fusion occurs when two elements combine to create a new element and, simultaneously, release a tremendous amount of energy. Rather than converting one form of energy into another, the reaction instead creates *new* energy. Fusion is one of the most powerful and energy-efficient processes known to the world; we race to find a means to safely harness its potential in the service of humanity.

Free Market Fusion is both a process and its result. It is a process that creates new products, services, and solutions and is typically ensconced in new or modified concepts. Although portions of entire industries can be involved and permutations of participants can range widely, it is easiest to discuss the process by considering first a few examples that most clearly demonstrate the process and potential of Free Market Fusion.

Free Market Fusion is the coming together of two or more entities, one or more of which is characterized as a for-profit enterprise and one or more of which is characterized as an institutional, nonprofit, quasi-governmental, or governmental entity. For purposes of illustration, we'll call them *A entities* (for-profit) *and B entities* (institutional, nonprofit, etc.). The process culminates typically in the fusing of a portion, or possibly all, of the assets of one or more A entities with typically a portion, or possibly all, of the assets of one or more B entities. This relationship can be diagrammed as follows:

12   Free Market Fusion

Free Market Fusion Process

Although approaching Free Market Fusion may result in the formation of new enterprises, typically at the outset, existing organizations are the creators. Also, typically there is a background of need, concern, or opportunity common to the entities involved that generates support for resolution. The collaborative process inherent in Free Market Fusion can engender the tremendous release of energies that comes from looking at the world not as a miasma of intractable problems, but as an arena of challenges awaiting exploration, initiative, and solution.

WORKING TOGETHER

In the Free Market Fusion process, each entity contributes its particular strengths, agreed upon by both parties, to the project. For example, in a partnership between an entrepreneurial group and an institution, the entrepreneur might contribute the initial innovative idea as well as technological marketing expertise and significant risk assumption. The institution might contribute manpower, physical facilities, familiarity with the existing market, and perhaps acceptability.

Depending on the parties, some of those roles might be reversed. However, the purpose of the partnership is always to enable both parties to accomplish goals neither could attain alone — to create a solution where there was none. As in a fusion process, the new solution is accompanied by a breathtaking burst of energy as new possibilities and opportunities open up to everyone involved in the process, both those creating the solution and those benefiting from it.

Knowledge TV, discussed in Chapter 5, provides an example of the Free Market Fusion process. The entrepreneurial entity in this case was Jones International, a company involved in cable television and various other communications entities. The institutional partner was a selection from the U.S.'s higher education community, 3,400 colleges and universities.

The problem (or opportunity) confronting higher education in the United States was that the size and nature of its constituency, plus work force requirements and education costs were changing much faster than the institutions themselves could respond. Enrollment of traditional students, fresh out of high school and committed to graduating from college within four years, was decreasing. Non-traditional students who were older, working, often with family commitments, were requesting alternative programs geared to their varied schedules and financial constraints.

The solution to this dilemma was to offer high-quality, college-level, for-credit courseware from colleges and universities across the country to students in their homes, offices, or libraries. In effect, it delivered education to the students, rather than the students to education. This diminishes the distance and time required to acquire education. And, for students who could afford tuition but not the added expense of on-campus room and board and affiliated student costs, Knowledge TV offered a way to make higher education financially accessible.

FREE MARKET FUSION, ENTREPRENEURS, AND INSTITUTIONS

A productive type of Free Market Fusion results from combining the strengths, resources, and assets of an institutional entity with those of an entrepreneurial group. In this situation, the strengths of the institution might include specialized subject knowledge, existing facilities, a thorough understanding of a specific market, a strong administrative and management structure, and a history of solid, stable functioning.

143

The strengths and assets of the entrepreneur might include expertise in competitive strategies, the ability to evaluate risks and a willingness to undertake intelligent ones, commitment to innovative thinking, awareness of opportunities presented by recent technological advances, strategic networking abilities, an understanding of and familiarity with capitalization resources, and the ability to orchestrate concepts into products.

The catalyst is leadership, which may or may not be provided by the free-wheeling entrepreneur. The obvious fact that an entrepreneur may be well known and accustomed to operating in the public spotlight does not mean that person will assume the leadership mantle, or that he or she should.

Leadership encompasses much more than simply assuming the role of primary public spokesperson. The most critical leadership activities are intuition, imagination, planning, organizing, networking, and acting as missionary within the organizations involved, persuading and recruiting supporters internally for a new concept. Often individuals with established credibility within an institution can do this most effectively. The entrepreneur may assume some parts of this role or merely advise and be an "outside" networker, promoting the concept to other organizations and individuals whose support is essential. Even the process of leadership may be shared or fused.

Entrepreneurs and institutions provide an especially effective example of Free Market Fusion because the combination enables them to combine many of their core strengths to accomplish what neither could accomplish alone.

INSTITUTIONS: INERTIA VERSUS INITIATIVE

Institutions are a critical part of society's infrastructure. They include schools, colleges and universities, hospitals, prisons, the military services, national charitable organizations, unions and professional organizations, quasi-governmental agencies, and such community entities as libraries, symphonies, museums, civic leagues, and innumerable religious groups. Often, they have existing physical facilities and a stable organizational structure. Successful institutions have a thorough understanding both of their constituencies and of those constituencies' special needs and concerns. Often they bring the comfort of market acceptance because of their involvement in the new solution.

Institutions play an important role in reaffirming our sense of community, especially today when we are deluged with an onslaught of change on a regular basis. As connections to our past, they are familiar and comforting. Many of them have been in existence almost as long as the country itself; others grew with the needs of our growing nation. Harvard was established in 1636, Yale in 1701, and in 1862 the Morrill Act led to the establishment of the public higher education system. Today, the United States has some 3,400 institutions of higher learning.

The first lending libraries in the U.S. were founded by English clergyman Thomas Bray in Maryland in the late 1600s, and the country's public library system was launched nationally when Andrew Carnegie undertook funding the construction of 2,500 community library buildings between 1881 and 1891. Some 5,400 public libraries now are supported by communities across the United States.

The Boy Scout and Girl Scout programs, originating in Great Britain, were introduced in the United States in the first decade of the 20th century and now involve well over 7 million children, teens, and adults. The YMCA, now with 25 million members in more than 90 countries, has been a pillar of thousands of communities since its inception in London in 1844; and community hospitals have been relied upon in U.S. towns and cities ever since Philadelphia's Pennsylvania Hospital first received its charter in 1751 through the tireless efforts of Benjamin Franklin.

Certainly institutions have played a central role in advancing the goals of society throughout history. It is imperative that they remain as vital and forward-thinking as possible if they are to continue their positive impact on society. This is no easy task: It is in the nature of institutions (and of monopolistic businesses) that stability may deteriorate to stagnation and management to mediocrity. Even Thomas Jefferson recognized this possibility, when he wrote:

> I am not an advocate for frequent change in laws or constitutions. But laws and institutions must go hand in hand with the progress of the human mind. As that becomes more developed, more enlightened, as new discoveries are made, new truths discovered and manners and opinions change, with the change of circumstances, institutions must advance also to keep pace

with the times. We might as well require a man to wear still the coat which fitted him when a boy as civilized society to remain ever under the regimen of their barbarous ancestors.[1]

Over the past several decades, we as a society seem to have lost confidence in the ability of our institutions to perform with competence and integrity the functions for which they were created. As circumstances have changed, often institutions have failed to change with them, choosing instead to hold onto the more familiar, less-threatening solutions of yesterday and to be protected by the environment that depended upon them.

The tendency of institutions and large organizations to rely on solutions drawn from yesterday's realities was pointed out some two decades ago by Peter Drucker in his article "Managing the Public Service Institution":

> No success lasts "forever." Yet it is even more difficult to abandon yesterday's success than it is to reappraise failure. Success breeds its own hubris. It creates emotional attachments, habits of thought and action, and, above all, false self-confidence. A success that has outlived its usefulness may, in the end, be more damaging than failure. Especially in a service institution, yesterday's success becomes "policy," "virtue," "conviction," if not indeed "Holy Writ," unless the institution imposes on itself the discipline of thinking through its mission, its objectives, and its priorities, and of building in feedback control from results over policies, priorities, and action.[2]

RISK-TAKING: THE KEY ROLE

A complementary relationship that can develop between entre-preneurs and partnering institutions relates to risk-taking. Mis-steps within an institutional environment can easily spell the end of a promising career, a circumstance that has an obvious (and under-

147

standable) dampening effect on an institutional leader's willingness to take risks. In addition to identifying opportunities, then, another of the entrepreneur's key roles in a Free Market Fusion venture is to assume a substantial amount of the risk involved in any new undertaking, thus diverting a large measure of the "exposure" from the institution's leader onto the entrepreneur.

COMBINING RISK-TAKING AND CAUTION

This imposes no hardship, for although risk-taking is anathema to an institution, judicious and well-informed risk-taking is second nature to the entrepreneur. An entrepreneur has the freedom to respond to opportunity with a desire for gain rather than resisting it because of a fear of loss. Similarly, because entrepreneurs are not part of the "old guard" operating environment of the institution and have minimal vested interests in conforming to established ideologies, they are much freer to envision radical alternatives and innovative solutions outside the boundaries of accepted practices.

Thomas Jefferson believed that every generation needed its own revolution. In the United States, entrepreneurs have always been society's revolutionaries, playing from outside the boundaries, creating new solutions for a changing world. Now they have an opportunity to chart new ground once again.

Exploring this "new frontier" will take discipline and commitment to a common vision, because the gains to be won through society's revitalization will be more long term than immediate. No work is more critical, however, for the well-being of the world; we simply cannot continue to exist, let alone compete fairly in the global marketplace, if major portions of our peoples or our infrastructures are left to perish in the wastelands of yesterday's solutions.

MODELING FREE MARKET FUSION

The major components of any Free Market Fusion process are:

1. Identifying and evaluating potential Free Market Fusion opportunities.
2. Creating an innovative solution.
3. Identifying potential partners.
4. Structuring the relationship.
5. Undertaking the project.

Obviously, every situation will demand different levels of time and energy at each phase. However, if participants know going into an undertaking that there is a process to work through, then resources can be allocated accordingly.

If an innovative solution incorporates a fairly non-traditional concept, it will be easier to work with a partner who already is comfortable with the non-traditional concept. For example, Knowledge TV combined a non-traditional delivery process (cable television) with a non-traditional teaching method (telecourses). The colleges and universities that had not previously used telecourses were not nearly as likely to be comfortable with the concept represented by Knowledge TV as were the schools that understood the potential of telecourses and had already integrated them effectively into their programs.

Another consideration is that many potential partners may be constrained by people or organizations whose vested interests might be threatened by the entity's move into a new arena or into a relationship with another (autonomous) entity where the vested interests have no control. A major contributor to the organization, for example, may forbid it from entering into any new relationship for fear that the contributor will lose his or her tacit control of the organization's goals and direction.

This is a fairly predictable response. Fear of change is a familiar reaction, especially for constituencies, such as labor union memberships or government or large business entities, which fear they may lose previously protected positions. Therefore it becomes critical to strive for an acceptable level of friction, whereby even though fear of change may be present, it is counterbalanced by enthusiastic commitment to the opportunity at hand.

This control relationship may not surface initially, but when it does it often terminates further negotiation.

STRUCTURING THE RELATIONSHIP

Once the concept of a Free Market Fusion combination is developed, then the manner in which these entities and related functions, equipment, personnel, or activities can be joined must be considered. What are the costs? Who must contribute what? Who might feel threatened? Who will manage the process? What kind of time frame will it take for Free Market Fusion to function? What are the risks involved and who will take them? What is the reward system? The list of potential questions to be answered is long and will vary with each project.

Obviously, each project will have its own set of circumstances and concerns that need to be addressed and agreed upon before other steps can be taken. However, the following areas can serve as a starting point from which to explore and negotiate.

Goal issues. What are the purposes and goals of this project? How will goals be measured? How and when will they be evaluated? What is the reward structure?

Inertia issues. Best-laid plans can easily be derailed by organizational inertia. How rapidly will both parties be able to respond to opportunities and/or crises? How rapidly are both parties *willing* to respond?

Structural and logistics issues. How will the project be undertaken? Where and how will it be located: centralized with one participant, headquartered at a project site, other? Who will implement what aspects of the project?

What is a reasonable and mutually agreeable time frame? This can become a key issue if both parties do not understand and accept how long it will take to accomplish key tasks. If the project will entail working with large institutions, government agencies, or other bureaucracies, (including bureaucratic businesses) the time from start to completition could be substantially extended..

Competition issues. How will you deal with competing players? Will you work around their established programs, trying not to disrupt their "market share," or will you try to displace their "product" with your own.

When dealing with societal concerns, much care must be taken around this issue. Society is rarely damaged when, in the rough-and-tumble competitive market of consumer goods, a candy bar or a laundry detergent or a sports car line bites the dust. However, when addressing societal issues, often a less-than-terrific solution is worth keeping because it provides ancillary benefits.

Long-term issues. Assuming the project is successful in meeting its goals and is profitable, what should become of it in the long-term? Should the relationship between the participants continue as is, or should it be reviewed on a specified basis? Should the project continue in its current form or be taken over by one of the participants? Be taken public as an established company? Move into other Free Market Fusion arenas?

CANDIDATES FOR FREE MARKET FUSION

There are many areas where a Free Market Fusion approach currently is or soon will be enabling us to make more creative, effective use of the technological tools now available. A few examples:

Health Care. It has become clear over the past several years that the world's health care crisis is going to demand radical measures and innovative solutions. The twin goals of cost containment and universal access to basic levels of medical care will obviously remain mutually exclusive unless efficient, cost-effective alternatives can be developed and implemented rapidly. A Free Market Fusion process combining the strengths and knowledge of the medical establishment with the vision and technological savvy of entrepreneurs offers the likeliest means of achieving these goals.

A scarcity of physicians in impoverished areas of many major cities as well as in the world's geographically isolated rural areas makes delivery of even the most basic, preventive medical care difficult if not impossible. But recent advances in two fields — remote diagnosis and home medical testing — are proving that quality health care and reasonable costs can go hand in hand.

Remote diagnosis, incorporating advances in computers and telecommunications, enables communities to avail themselves of state-of-the-art medical technological expertise well beyond the means of their local medical practitioner. In addition, when communities, whether geographically remote or inner-city, can avail themselves of these technologies only as necessary, it allows them to focus resources on basic medical care provided by less-costly medical professionals such as paramedics and nurse practitioners.

Like remote diagnosis, home health screening, medical testing and diagnostic technology can offer us the opportunity to save time, money, and lives. In addition, innovations in medication-delivery tools are enabling patients to self-administer oxygen, shots, and even intravenous food through a pump carried in a small nylon backpack. These products and services have been developed by medical entrepreneurs who saw better ways of meeting individuals' health care needs.

Environment. Over 25 years have passed since the first Earth Day, in April 1970, called the world's attention to the deteriorating state of the global environment. Since that first tolling bell of warning, we have become increasingly familiar with the challenges that confront us. Global warming and its greenhouse effect have continued unabated as waste gases, primarily carbon dioxide released by the combustion of oil, coal, and gas, continue to spew into the Earth's atmosphere. These same energy sources will one day be expended. Meanwhile, the world's waters and aquatic species are still being poisoned by acid rain, largely the result of sulfur dioxide released into the air by coal-burning power plants. The Earth-circling ozone layer is less and less able to protect us from the life-threatening effects of the sun's ultraviolet rays as chlorofluorocarbons (CFCs) continue to eat away at this protective blanket. In tropical regions of the Third World, growing populations desperate for economic survival burn their forests to clear enough land to graze cattle or cultivate marketable crops, taking more and more tropical rain forests out of the increasingly precarious global ecological balance. The industrialized world's reliance on non-renewable resources simply guarantees the ongoing acceleration of these frightening trends.

Technology has enabled a multitude of innovative environmental solutions across a broad range of targets. Alternative, renewable energy sources such as solar photovoltaic cells, geothermal and solar-thermal generation, wind power, and hydrogen are no longer dismissed as fringe thinking. "Industrial ecology" is becoming the manufacturing credo of the 1990s, as more and more companies understand that by redesigning manufacturing processes they are able to avoid using materials that end up as toxic waste, and thereby to avoid the costs associated with toxic material disposal or storage.

Sustainable development is a goal we all must embrace. It is imperative to accept the fact that market-based environmentalism offers the most effective means of transferring technological advances into the areas of greatest need, ensuring that future generations will inherit a land, not a landfill.

Public Television. The outstanding but beleaguered U.S. Public Broadcasting System (PBS) now faces an array of circumstances that may cause it to change its vision and even create a new mission. PBS is finding itself in an increasingly competitive environment due to the types of educational and cultural programming now available through cable television.

In 1991, the Corporation for Public Broadcasting (CPB) commissioned an outside management study by the Boston Consulting Group, which recognized the changing TV broadcast environment and the necessity for programming changes and new funding strategies. The study laid out a strategic approach to making change.[3]

A separate and independent study and report released in 1993 by the Twentieth Century Fund was more comprehensive in its analysis and more complimentary in its praise of PBS's quality programming contributions. This study was also extremely demanding of change for PBS in recognition of the changes in the TV industry, the need for more and better true educational programming, and the financial climate of the 1990s.[4]

Though almost all of PBS's programming is sometimes labeled as "educational," it is instructive to examine what resources are actually earmarked for certified TV education courses. The total revenues for the entire Public Broadcasting System, from the Corporation for Public Broadcasting down to the local stations' fund-raising drives, was $1.5 billion[5] in 1994. From that total, $137 million was devoted to all educational programming, of which $8.2 million went to for-credit college telecourses. The $8.2 million represented one-half of one percent (0.5%)[6] of total public television expenditures, indicating that college credit telecourses are a relatively minor part of PBS programming.

13 PBS PROGRAMMING MIX, 1994

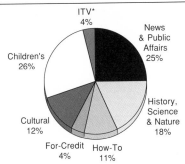

Typical Large Market
PBS Station

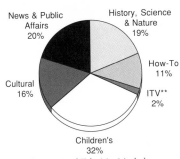

Typical Small Market
PBS Station

*ITV (Instructional Television) includes programming for K-12 classroom use and Cable in the Classroom.

**ITV (Instructional Television) includes programming for K-12 classroom use, Cable in the Classroom, and a minimal amount of for-credit courses (under 1%).

Source: Malarkey-Taylor Associates, 1995

While public television serves many masters other than ITV, consider the possibilities for instructional programming delivery if some of the CPB and PBS's annual overhead budgets — close to $60 million annually in some years — could be redirected to acquire additional for-credit education programming. Clearly, as long as it is governmentally funded, public debate is appropriate and opportunities for Free Market Fusion exist within the PBS mission.

CHALLENGES ARE PLENTIFUL

The list of challenges we face is long and daunting. A quick hit list of social concerns might include the high dropout rate for high school minorities, illiteracy, child poverty, drug addiction, a rising crime rate, AIDS, homelessness, overcrowded prisons, and a sky-high recidivism rate, increasing the level of effectiveness and accessibility (financial as well as logistic) for our higher education resources, re-incorporating seniors into productive societal roles, mainstreaming the physically handicapped back into society so that they can live independent lives and make the contributions they are capable of, and adequate, affordable medical care.

The world is caught in a web of suffering that decades of goodwill, foreign aid, and well-intentioned but often fruitless efforts have failed to eradicate. The world hunger problem and its companion issues, overpopulation and poorly managed resources, seem by now incapable of solution. Yet are they?

Where do we begin? *How* do we begin? We can begin with Free Market Fusion.

THE LARGER ARENA: TAPPING ENTREPRENEURIAL TALENT

Why not go to the world's entrepreneurs and ask them for solutions? These are individuals trained to see the opportunities in change, the possibilities in dislocation. Not as constrained by governmental structures or established processes, entrepreneurs are free to find the most effective ways to meet goals. Who knows what re-ordering of existing resources, what re-thinking of current responses, we might achieve? We need to tap the creative energy and risk-taking spirit of those willing to operate in Buckminster Fuller's "outlaw area" of untried solutions and no guarantees.

I believe solutions are always possible. The key for us is to structure the circumstances that nurture creative, innovative thinking so that our most innovative thinkers can design new solutions. For it is obvious that when a society faces a problem that has continually resisted traditional means of resolution, other solutions must be invented and tried. It becomes necessary to think and create outside the structure of established assumptions and policies *with great speed.*

The challenges that have been described in this book and with which higher education must deal are formidable. What has become obvious is that the changes will occur. People who want higher education will find a way to get it and, with rapidly opening free markets, there will be suppliers.

The challenge of our world's higher education establishment is to accept this inevitable shift in its student market, to identify partners and technologies which will help it respond, and to set about, perhaps through Free Market Fusion, creating ways to be more effective education suppliers in the 21st century.

---

[1]Thomas Jefferson, letter to Samuel Kercheval, 12 July 1816.

[2]Peter Drucker, *Innovation and Entrepreneurship: Principles and Practice* (New York: Harper & Row, 1985), 17.

[3]Corporation for Public Broadcasting, *Strategies for Public Television in a Multi-channel Environment: The Boston Consulting Group Study* (Washington, D.C.: March 1991).

[4]The Report of the Twentieth Century Fund Task Force on Public Television, *Quality Time?* (New York: The Twentieth Century Fund Press, 1993)

[5]Malarkey-Taylor Associates, *PBS Telecourse Study* (Washington, D.C.: May 1995).

[6]Malarkey-Taylor Associates, *Research Study on Public Broadcasting* (Washington, D.C.: March 1995).

Tut, tut, child, said the Duchess. Everything's got a moral if only you can find it.

—Lewis Carroll,
Alice's Adventures in Wonderland

Epilogue

The information revolution is ending. Long live the age of knowledge.

As some unnamed sage once quipped, "successful revolutions hasten their own demise." This view couldn't more aptly describe what has happened to the much heralded information revolution, which has marked our world's passing from the industrial to the post-industrial era, or more appropriately, the knowledge age.

Second in importance only to the changes brought about by a revolution are its artifacts, which represent the catalysts of change.

The valuable artifacts of the American Revolution are not its military paraphernalia but the colonial printing presses and the information media they produced: Letters, newspapers, pamphlets, extracts of sermons and speeches and, that singular document, the Declaration of Independence. Many of the documents pre-dated the actual hostilities, or, in the case of the Declaration, clarified for posterity the passions that were unleashed after almost two decades of dissent and protest in the American colonies.

Never in the history of mankind had political discussion and debate been so effectively or spontaneously communicated as in the outpouring of political rhetoric flowing from the colonial presses. Thousands of cheap leaflets and pamphlets were printed, passed hand-to-hand, and reprinted so that the 13 colonies were literally papered with the ideas of democracy.

When future anthropologists sift through the artifacts of the information revolution, they will come across the skeletal outlines of electronic platforms — the new communications organizations of the late 20th century that have made our swift transition into the age of knowledge possible.

Electronic platforms are neurological in nature. In many ways they resemble the human brains they feed. They combine many concepts, pieces of circuitry, extensive delivery facilities, and content connected in neurological fashion. They are interconnected to act in concert and, as more and more connectivity evolves, the platforms become broader and deeper.

As electronic media, they look much like cable, telecommunications and computer-based entities. They are transitory, morphing, enabling organizations that act as creators and purveyors of information, entertainment and education. These evolving electronic platforms are changing, among other things, the nature of knowledge enablement, especially teaching models as they have existed since the days of early Athens.

At the moment of this writing, electronic platforms are transforming the globe's education systems into cyberschools where knowledge is transformed into video and other electronic media textbooks, lectures, demonstrations, and e-mail chat sessions among faculty and students. For those societies that are wealthy, the transition is coming almost overnight. For those that are poor, it is coming more slowly, but the wave of change is as inevitable as the wave of illiteracy eradication that has swept the world in the past 10 years.

Electronic platforms not only guarantee delivery, they assure standards of excellence and act as a potent weapon against censorship and information control. They provide a level playing field, assuring that students who enter a cyberschool immediately have at their disposal vast resources of electronically stored and linked information resources which can quickly put them on a par with their contemporaries. These resources, combined with a willingness to manipulate them appropriately, also place the cyberstudent in the unique position of being able to question and challenge assumptions and hypotheses as never before.

The overlying contribution of cyberschools, and this includes such early innovators as the publicly funded Sunrise Semester and Star Schools, the private Knowledge TV and the existing and growing number of open universities adopting electronic delivery, is that they provide a transfer of power to individuals. This power enables individuals to transform their own lives, regardless of whether they live in the rural reaches of the American West, the

West, the Australian outback, or in the great, densely populated cities of South America and Asia.

While economic wherewithal to access the electronic platform technology is still an obstacle to the world's poor, this obstruction will be circumvented in a few short years by a new wave of cheap, universally accessible electronic platforms and networks that will finally transform virtually every setting that has electric power — living rooms, one-room school houses, and, yes, even one-room huts — into access points for the age of knowledge.

Education through electronic platforms has the added advantage of efficient delivery. Such delivery systems are free of much of the friction of traditional education and government bureaucracy which once kept education the exclusive domain and source of power for the elite. Quality assurance will remain an important part of institutional oversight, but accrediting organizations will change the way they view students and institutions.

Electronic platforms provide an augmentation to the world's education systems in the late 20th century, but they will quickly emerge as the only economical solution to satisfy the increased global demand for education in the 21st century that is documented in the first chapter of this book. Importantly, they can provide "scale" of delivery and market access for educational solutions such as cyberschools. Still, no one existing institution, company or industry can do it all; there is room for all to participate.

For educators who are reluctant to accept electronic education delivery because of its unavoidable assault on cultural icons, I offer the assurance of philosophers from McLuhan to Plato. As McLuhan observed, TV — and we can extend this to electronic platforms of all kinds — created a new environment through which we observe the "old" environment of the industrial age, helping us understand and learn from it. Likewise, the industrial age turned the Renaissance into an art form because of the new perspective by which it could be viewed. Plato, the scribe of Athens when writing was new, turned oral dialogue into art by documenting it.

It is my conviction that the technology and communications revolutions are propelling us into a new Renaissance, the knowledge age. This age will accelerate as the private side of our world economy and cultural life entwine with the world's great problems and we begin to perceive them as opportunities, especially in education. The outcome can be a more peaceful world, a diverse vibrant world alive with new levels of expectations.

One of the evolving but ultimately predominant artifacts of the knowledge age will be cyberschools. Long live the age of knowledge.

Glenn R. Jones
December 1996

All that ever stays the same is change.

— *I Ching*

APPENDIX A — Principles for Distance Learning

THE WESTERN INTERSTATE COMMISSION FOR HIGHER EDUCATION'S (WICHE) PRINCIPLES OF GOOD PRACTICE FOR ELECTRONICALLY OFFERED ACADEMIC DEGREE AND CERTIFICATE PROGRAMS.

The following is the complete text of the WICHE principles.

Preamble

These principles are the product of a Western Cooperative for Educational Telecommunications project, "Balancing Quality and Access: Reducing State Policy Barriers to Electronically Delivered Higher Education Programs."

The three-year project, supported by the U.S. Department of Education's Fund for the Improvement of Postsecondary Education, is designed to foster an interstate environment that encourages the electronic provision of quality higher education programs across state lines. The principles have been developed by a group representing the Western states higher education regulating agencies, higher education institutions, and the regional accrediting community.

Recognizing that the context for learning in our society is undergoing profound changes, those charged with developing the principles have tried not to tie them to or compare them to, traditional campus structures. The principles are also designed to be sufficiently flexible that institutions offering a range of programs — from graduate degree to certificates — will find them useful.

Several assumptions form the basis for these principles:

- The electronically offered program is provided by or through an institution that is accredited by a nationally recognized accrediting body.

- The institution's programs holding specialized accreditation meet the same requirements when offered electronically.

- The institution may be a traditional higher education institution, a consortium of such institutions, or another type of organization or entity.

- The principles address programs rather than individual courses.

- It is the institution's responsibility to review educational programs it provides via technology in terms of its own internal definitions of these principles.

PRINCIPLES

Curriculum and Instruction

1. Each electronically offered program of study results in learning outcomes appropriate to the rigor and breadth of the degree or certificate awarded.

2. An electronically offered degree or certificate program is coherent and complete.

3. The program provides for appropriate real-time or delayed interaction between faculty and students and among students.

4. Qualified faculty provide appropriate oversight of the program electronically offered.

Institutional Context and Commitment to Role and Mission

5. The program is consistent with the institution's role and mission.

6. Review and approval processes ensure the appropriateness of the technology being used to meet the program's objectives.

Faculty Support

7. The program provides faculty support services specifically related to teaching via an electronic system.

8. The program provides training for faculty who teach via the use of technology.

Resources for Learning

9. The program ensures appropriate learning resources are available to students.

Students and Student Services

10. The program provides students with clear, complete, and timely information on the curriculum, course and degree requirements, nature of faculty/student interaction, assumptions about technological competence and skills, technical equipment requirements, availability of academic support services and financial aid resources, and costs and payment policies.

11. The enrolled students have reasonable and adequate access to the range of student services appropriate to support their learning. That accepted students have the background, knowledge, and technical skills needed to undertake the program.

12. Advertising, recruiting, and admissions materials clearly and accurately represent the program and the services available.

Commitment to Support

13. Policies for faculty evaluation include appropriate consideration of teaching and scholarly activities related to electronically offered programs.

14. The institution demonstrates a commitment to ongoing support, both financial and technical, and to continuation of the program for a period sufficient to enable students to complete a degree/certificate.

Evaluation and Assessment

15. The institution evaluates the program's educational effectiveness, including assessments of student learning outcomes, student retention, and student and faculty satisfaction.

16. Students have access to such program evaluation data.

17. The institution provides for assessment and documentation of student achievement in each course and at completion of the program.[1]

THE AMERICAN COUNCIL ON EDUCATION, CENTER FOR ADULT LEARNING AND EDUCATIONAL CREDENTIALS' GUIDING PRINCIPLES FOR DISTANCE LEARNING IN A LEARNING SOCIETY

The following is the complete text of the American Council on Education's Guiding Principles for Distance Learning, including a statement of the principles' core values. (Draft released May 1996.)

CORE VALUES

These principles assume that the practice of distance learning contributes to the larger social mission of education and training in a democratic society. With that in mind, the principles reflect the following tenets and values:

- Learning is a lifelong process, important to successful participation in the social, cultural, civic, and economic life of a democratic society.

- Lifelong learning involves the development of a range of learning skills and behaviors that should be explicit outcomes of learning activities.

- The diversity of learners, learning needs, learning context, and modes of learning must be recognized if the learning activities are to achieve their goals.

- All members of society have the right to access learning opportunities that provide the means for effective participation in society.

- Participation in a learning society involves both rights and responsibilities for learners, providers, and those charged with the oversight of learning.

- Because learning is social and sensitive to context, learning experiences should support interaction and the development of learning communities, whether social, public, or professional.

- The development of a learning society may require significant changes in the roles, responsibilities, and activities of provider organizations and personnel as well as of the learners themselves.

PRINCIPLES

1. Distance learning activities are designed to fit the specific context for learning.

   a) Learning opportunities include a clear statement of intended learning outcomes, learning content that is appropriate to those outcomes, clear expectations of learner activities, flexible opportunities for interactions, and assessment methods appropriate to the activities and technologies.

b) Elements of a learning event — the learning content, instructional methods, technologies, and context — complement each other.

c) The selection and application of technologies for a specific learning opportunity are appropriate for the intended learning outcomes, subject matter content, relevant characteristics and circumstances of the learner, and cost range.

d) Learning activities and modes of assessment are responsible to the learning needs of individual learners.

e) The learning experience is organized to increase learner control over the time, place, and pace of instruction.

f) Learning outcomes address both content mastery and increased learning skills.

g) Individuals with specialized skills in content, instructional methods, or technologies work collaboratively as a design team to create learning opportunities.

h) The learning design is evaluated on a regular basis for effectiveness, with findings utilized as a basis for improvement.

2. Distance learning opportunities are effectively supported for learners through fully accessible modes of delivery and resources.

a) The providing organization has a learner support system to assist the learner in effectively using the resources provided. This system includes technology and technical support, site facilitation, library and information services, advising, counseling, and problem-solving assistance.

b) The provider considers the needs for learner support in relation to the distance learning mode(s) used and makes provision for delivery of appropriate resources based on the design of the learning activities, the technology involved, and the needs of the learner.

c) Access to support services — such as scheduling, registration, and record keeping — is convenient, efficient, and responsive to diverse learners as well as consistent with other elements of the delivery system.

d) Support systems are accessible to and usable by the learners and are sufficiently flexible to accommodate different learning styles.

e) The provider discloses to the learner all information pertinent to the learning opportunity — such as course prerequisites, modes of study, evaluation criteria, and technical needs — and provides some form of orientation for those desiring it.

f) Support systems for learning opportunity are reviewed regularly to ensure their currency and effectiveness.

3. Distance learning initiatives must be backed by an organizational commitment to quality and effectiveness in all aspects of the learning environment.

a) Involvement in distance learning is consistent with the overall mission of the provider; policies regarding distance learning are integrated into the provider's overall policy framework.

b) The providing organization makes a financial and administrative commitment to maintain distance learning programs through completion and to support faculty and learner services needed to ensure an effective learning environment.

c) Administrative and support systems (registration, advising, assessment, etc.) are compatible with the learning delivery system to ensure a coherent learning environment.

d) The organization's curricular and administrative policies incorporate the needs of distance learning as well as traditional learning activities.

e) The provider makes a commitment to research and development of distance learning, maintaining a systematic evaluation of the content, processes, and support systems involved in its distance learning activities.

f) The provider makes a concomitant investment of resources and effort in professional development and support of both faculty and staff involved in distance learning.

g) The providing organization recognizes effective participation in distance learning in its promotion and reward system for faculty and staff and ensures that its policies regarding promotion, tenure (if applicable), and departmental/program funding reflect the integration of distance learning into the organization's mission.

h) The policies, management practices, learning design process, and operational procedures for distance learning are regularly evaluated to ensure effectiveness and currency.

i) The provider does not distinguish between learning accomplished at a distance and learning accomplished through other means in recognizing learner achievement.

4. Distance education programs organize learning activities around demonstrable learning outcomes, assist the learner to achieve these outcomes, and assess learner progress by reference to these outcomes.

a) When possible, individual learners help shape the learning outcomes and how they are achieved.

b) Intended learning outcomes are described in observable, measurable, and achievable terms.

c) The learning design is consistent with and shaped to achieve the intended learning outcomes.

d) Distance education media and delivery systems are used in a way that facilitates the achievement of intended learning outcomes.

e) Learning outcomes are assessed in a way relevant to the content, the learner's situation, and the distance education delivery system.

f) Assessment of learning is timely, appropriate, and responsive to the needs of the learner.

g) Intended learning outcomes are reviewed regularly to assure their clarity, utility, and appropriateness for the learners.

5. The provider has a plan and infrastructure for using technology that support its learning goals and activities.

a) The technology plan defines the technical requirement and compatibility needed to support the learning activity.

b) The technology plan addresses system security to assure the integrity and validity of information shared in the learning activities.

c) The technology facilitates interactivity among all elements of a learning environment and places a high value on ease of use by learners.

d) The technology selected for distance learning is fully accessible and understandable to learners and has the power necessary to support its intended use.

e) Providers communicate the purpose of the technologies used for learning and, through training, assist learners, faculty, and staff to understand its etiquette, acquire the knowledge and skills to manipulate and interact with it, and understand the objectives and outcomes that the technologies are intended to support.

f) The technology infrastructure meets the needs of both learners and learning facilitators for presenting information, interacting within the learning community, and gaining access to learning resources.[2]

---

[1]Sally M. Johnstone and B. Krauth, "Some Principles of Good Practice for the Virtual University," *Change*, March–April 1996, 40.

[2]Eugene Sullivan and T. Rocco, co-chairs, Task Force on Distance Learning, "Guiding Principles for Distance Learning in a Learning Society," draft copy (May 1996), 3–5.

APPENDIX B — Internet Addresses

INTERNET ADDRESSES FOR INSTITUTIONS MENTIONED IN CYBERSCHOOLS: AN EDUCATION RENAISSANCE

Address	Institution
http://www.ACENET.edu	American Council on Education
http://www.research.apple.com/ research/proj/acot	Apple Classrooms of Tomorrow
http://www.open.ac.uk/	British Open University On-Line
http://www.webcom.com/~cyberhi	Cyber High School
http://www.uwex.edu/disted/home.html	Distance Education Clearing House
http://www.exen.com/	Executive Education Network
http://www.fielding.edu	The Fielding Institute
http://www.gsn.org	Global Schoolhouse
http://uu-gna.mit.edu:8001/uu-gna/ index.html	Globewide Network Academy
http://www.iuc.com	International University College
http://www.jec.edu/knonline/glp/gel.html	Jones' Global Electronic Library
http://www.digitallantern.com/McLuhan/	Marshall McLuhan
http://www.jec.edu	Knowledge TV
http://www.sistema.itesm.mx/	Monterrey Institute of Technology
http://rs6.loc.gov/amhome.html	National Digital Library (U.S. Library of Congress)
http://www.nlc-bnc.ca/	National Library of Canada
http://www.ntu.edu/	National Technological University
http://www.etc.bc.ca	New Directions in Distance Learning
http://www.oclc.org/oclc/	On-Line Computer Library Center
http://www.cde.psu.edu/de/catalog	Pennsylvania State University
http://www.tui.edu	The Union Institute
http://www.uophx.edu/	University of Phoenix

INDEX